WESSEX DIARIES

For David and Ann
with many
thanks and
happy memories

WESSEX DIARIES

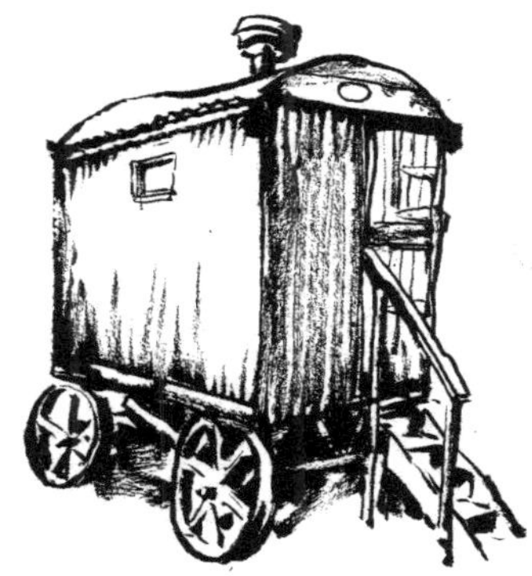

Sketches from life in Hardy Country

JOHN VALLINS

FLAGON PRESS

WESSEX DIARIES

First published in 2011
by Flagon Press
Forge House, Fore St,
Winsham, Chard
Somerset TA20 4DY

www.james-crowden.co.uk

A catalogue record for this book
is available from the British Library

ISBN 978-0-9562778-2-4

Typeset in ITC New Baskerville
Designed by Andrew Crane
Printed by Butler Tanner and Dennis
Frome, Somerset.

Published by Flagon Press in 2011

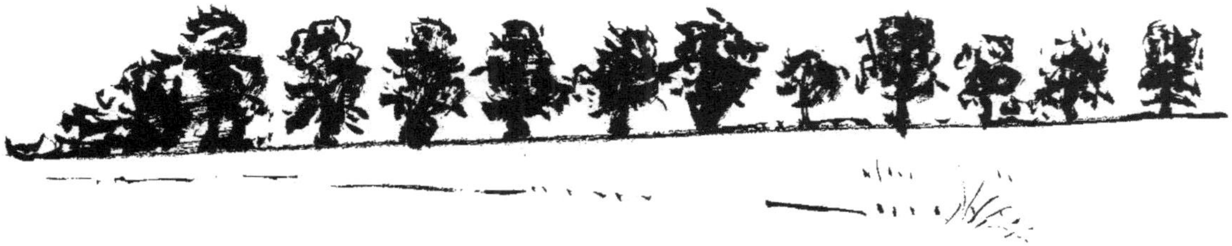

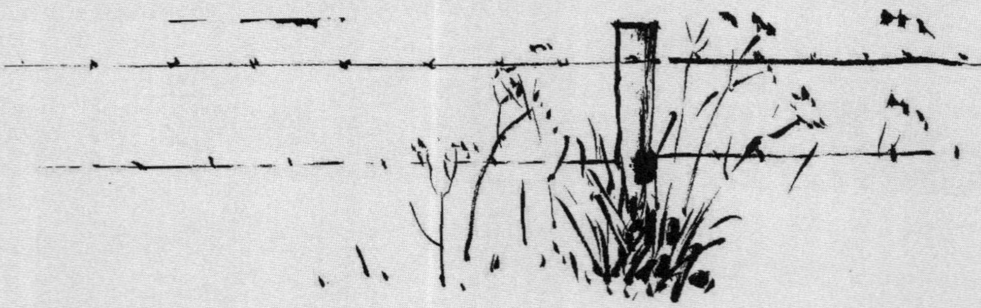

Contents

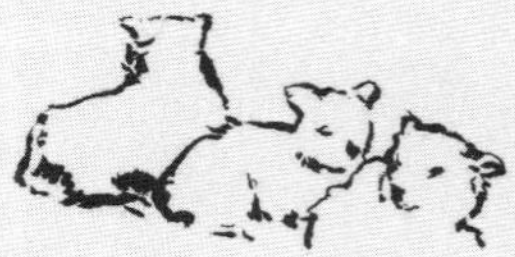

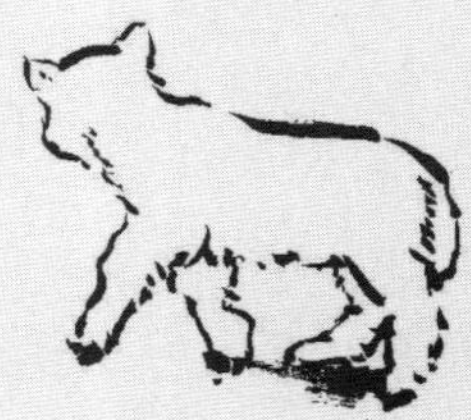

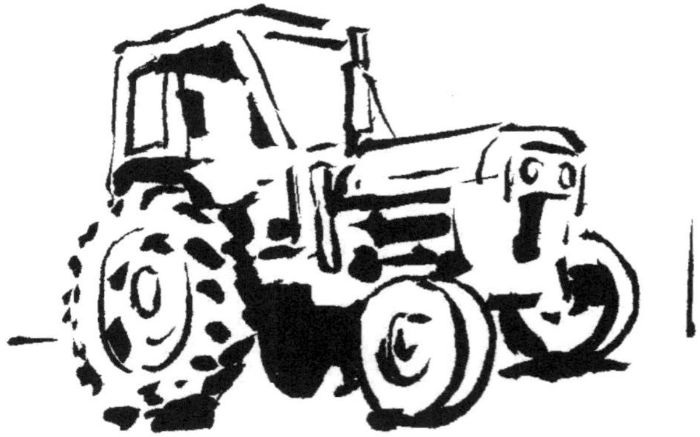

Acknowledgements

I would like to thank:

All those who have generously provided material for these 'diaries'; some are close friends, others I have met only once. They have told their stories, demonstrated their skills, or led us to people, places or events that we should not have found without their help.

Celia Locks, at *The Guardian*, who looks after the Country Diary with devoted care and has provided constant support.

Lisa Darnell and her colleagues at Guardian Books whose help has been invaluable.

Alan Rusbridger, editor of *The Guardian*, who has kindly contributed such a generous foreword.

Tim Millar, whose line expresses the character of our landscape with sympathy and economy.

James Crowden and his team, who have provided the encouragement and expertise to assemble and shape the parts to make this book.

My wife, Sallie, who has lived with the fortnightly rhythm and demands of Wessex Country Diaries for almost twenty years and shared most of the travels, experiences and conversations that underlie the contents.

J V

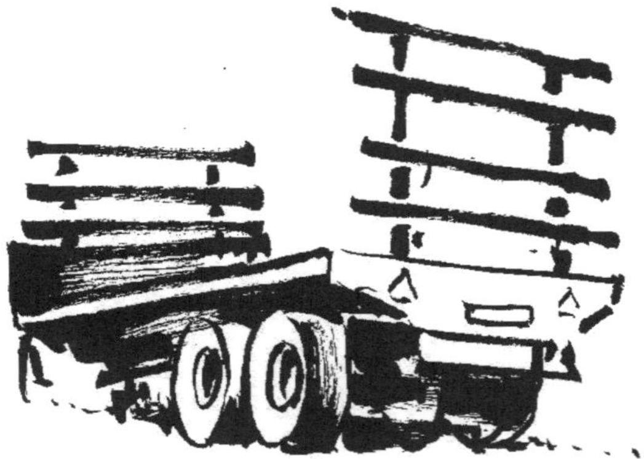

Foreword

Half a lifetime ago I had a rather inspiring English teacher, without whose erudition and encouragement I doubt I would have achieved much in life. He spotted a modest literary talent in me. But, more importantly, he opened my eyes into how writing worked.

He was a man of infectious enthusiasm. I think I mean that literally, in the sense that his excitement about a particular poet or novel was actually catching. I will give you one example – the day he bounded into class one day to tell a bunch of recalcitrant teenagers about a 19th century Northamptonshire nature poet.

He told us about John Clare's desperate life and times. There was something almost cinematic in his telling of Clare's long, three-day walk home from the Essex asylum where he'd been detained to meet his first love, Mary Joyce, only to discover she had died three years earlier. And then the teacher started on the poetry Clare had written in the 20-odd years he'd spent confined in the Northamptonshire County General Lunatic Asylum.

Looking back, I can think of no reason why the nature poems of a mentally-troubled labourer should have held any appeal to my 16-year old self, except for the narrative power, integrity and sheer literary conviction of John Vallins. Whatever the force, it had an extraordinary effect on me. I devoted my next school holiday to finding out all I could about Clare. I travelled to Northampton with a friend, stayed in a youth hostel, visited the town library to inspect their manuscripts and even made a pilgrimage to the lunatic asylum to interview the then superintendent. John had, knowingly or not, lit some kind of fire inside me.

Our paths barely crossed for at least two decades. And then, at some point, I was the editor of *The Guardian* and he was the soon-to-retire head of Chetham's Music School in Manchester. It must have been his suggestion that he might try his hand at country diaries in retirement in Somerset. I needed little convincing.

The Country Diary has been published in *The Guardian* for well over 100 years. In 2006 we published a collection, with the bold claim that it was "the longest-lasting uninterrupted column in British newspapers."

The compiler of that collection, Martin Wainwright, explained the reason for the column's longevity:

"The diary isn't ephemeral. Most journalism is (the word means 'of the day' and no one has achieved lasting fame through journalism alone); but the Country Diaries have lasted because they are such good natural history observation… The subject is everything. The British countryside is varied and lovely. No two days of weather are the same. British beasts and birds are fascinating… This is a more fundamental world than the goings-on in Whitehall or Baghdad, and not just as a calmer, sweeter alternative. The countryside is the frontier where Nature fights against exploitation, ultimately for our survival. Like scouts, the diarists bring back reports on the struggle…"

Wainwright's book quotes one of the great diarists, William Condry on the value of such diaries.

"For maybe sixty years a chap will write down a daily miscellany of what seem rather pointless observations about plants, birds, mammals, insects, fish ore merely the weather, pointless because he hardly ever refers to them again... they may lie neglected for half a century but eventually somebody feels inquisitive enough to dip into them. The dross of fifty years ago, like old bottles, has acquired an unexpected value… So, gathering his little daily store of notes, our diarist, without realising it, was writing a quite unique kind of history."

Condry was referring to a local naturalist in Aberystwyth, whose diaries he had stumbled upon in a library. But that phrase – "a unique kind of history" – could equally well be applied to John Vallins's collection of diaries about the patch of land around his home in Somerset.

That plain power of narrative which I'd experienced as a teenager is still there in John's simple writing. He is part naturalist; part journalist; part historian; part anthropologist. He makes little voyages of discovery around Somerset, revealing a form of rural English life that many townsfolk must have assumed died years ago. He stops and talks to country people, gently teasing out their stories. He researches the history and topography of the locality. He is as easy in describing buildings as he is in writing about the process of cider-making. His keen, warm eye finds fascination and humanity in the work of the blacksmith or the pig farmer, or the shepherd or the bell-hanger.

There have been some great Guardian country diarists in the history of the much-loved and read column. John Vallins is up there with the best of them and if this book is half as inspiring to a general reader as he was a teacher, then it will earn its place as a minor classic of the genre.

Alan Rusbridger

June 2011

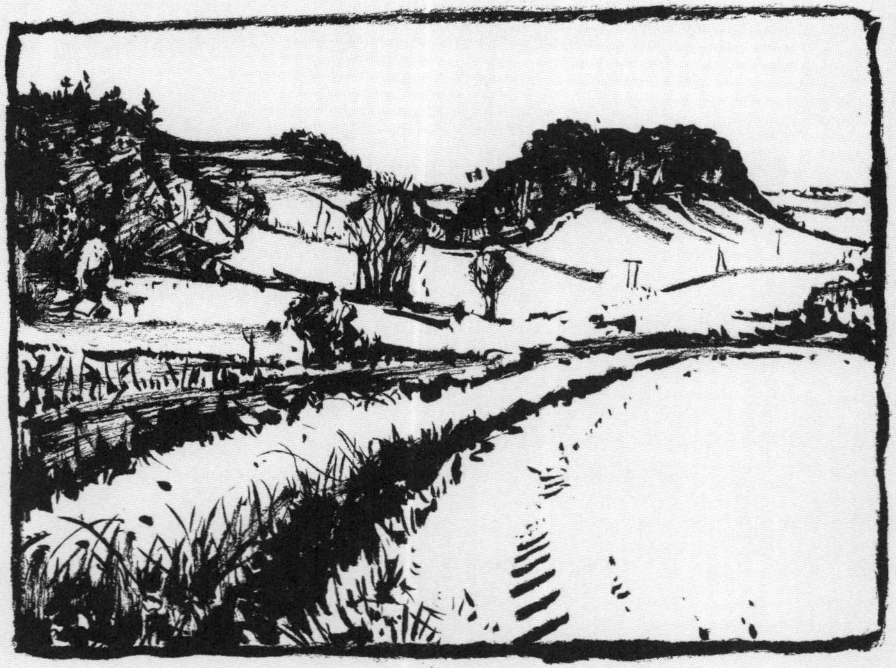

SPRING

Sheep Shearing

The millpond, stream and ditches were brimming over. Across Blackmore Vale, described by old-time writers as a tract of thicket and quagmire, there were sheets of water. The first batch of Dartmoor sheep were due for shearing on the Sunday, and the wet weather created difficulties.

Shearing heavy and shaggy Dartmoors is hard enough at the best of times. If the wool is wet it may be impossible, and damp fleeces go mouldy. And then, there is the welfare of the animals themselves. Deprived of their thermal, waterproof covering, they will suffer if the weather stays wet, and especially if the wind blows cold. So Sunday's batch of Dartmoors spent much of the week in the barn.

The shearing was to be done by a young couple from Dorset, dairy farmers who used to keep sheep, but switched to cows because the return on sheep is far smaller. But they like and understand sheep, and still travel to shear for friends with small flocks, often rare breeds bred for shows.

The first candidate was a five-year-old ram. They reckoned his weight at about two and a half hundredweight. It took twenty minutes of sweat and skill – heaving his bulk into position without hurting or antagonising him, talking to him in reassuring tones, working the shears down the belly of matted wool, over the rump, then flopping him over on first one side then the other to do legs, sides, head and back. It was an impressive combination of strength and precision, with miraculously deft movement over the tricky and delicate parts ('With show sheep or pets, I aim to leave the ears on').

Downland sheep are easy; the fleece comes off neatly in one piece like a readymade hearthrug. But thick, chunky Dartmoor wool comes off in an uneven bundle. As soon as he was shorn, the ram wandered outside, apparently unconcerned. There was no rain or cold wind. After a smallish ewe came the real challenge – Manifold, a ram of enormous bulk whose name derives from the number of his offspring. Despite a few vigorous demonstrations of resentment, he swallowed his pride and submitted.

Thatch

The appearance of the old Somerset Long House where we buy cider has been changing in recent weeks. The old thatch, black and weather-beaten, is being replaced by new, trim and yellow. Bundles of combed wheat-reed, the traditional thatching material in the South and West, are stacked below, bound and cut to size. Old thatch is taken off until a sound layer is uncovered; it may be original, hundreds of years old. The thatch can have a thickness of several feet, especially up towards the ridge, where extra layers may have been applied over time to produce a steeper pitch. New bundles are laid, knocked into place with a "bat" or "legget" made from a flat piece of wood studded with nails, and fixed with a hazel "spar", sharpened at each end and bent double like a hairpin. This particular long roof, with rounded eaves or "eyebrows" over dormer windows, will take three men four or five weeks to work. Local materials and methods produce the familiar soft contours and cushioned look which differ from the flatter, sharper effect seen in other regions. The ridge, with sculptured shapes, is strapped and knit together with long hazel "liggers" and more spars. The life of new thatch varies according to materials, conditions, situation, and the pitch of the roof. It may be 20 years, or it may be 40. If a lot of air gets to the roof, and not too much rain, it lasts longer. The windier the better. In the open spaces of East Anglia, where they use water-reed, which grows plentifully in Norfolk, thatch tends to last even longer. Amongst others, a group of small farmers near Ilminster cultivate long wheat reed specifically suited to thatching as a cash crop. They harvest it to traditional methods to preserve the length, and bind it for the market. People say thatching is a dying craft, but there are 25 thatchers listed in the Taunton Yellow Pages, ten members of the Somerset Thatching Association and newcomers trained by the Rural Development Commission.

The Grass Keep Auction

Since Easter, chilly winds have blown hard and more or less relentlessly across the hills, and the flatlands have been quagmires or lakes. On Creech Hill, if you leaned against the wind, it knocked you back the other way, and there was April snow on the Mendips. The growth of grass has been slow, and it was incongruous that the day of the first local 'grasskeep' sale was clear, dry, warm, and balmy. 'Grass Keep' is the system whereby a landowner lets out fields as grassfeed and mowing grass to farmers who need extra grazing and maybe want to take a cut of grass for silage. The price, payable in two instalments, one straight away and the other in August, allows the purchaser the use of the land 'to be grazed by accredited cattle or steers over six months old on November 8 with liberty to mow each lot once'. We walked the fields with the auctioneer, the owner and a dozen or so farmers. The auctioneer took his stance in each field and we formed a loose semi-circle. The printed schedule listed each lot's size and characteristics – access, good fencing, watering by trough from the mains, crossed by footpath (no bulls) and so on. The auctioneer extolled its specially desirable qualities, and dug in a heel to support his claim that the land was already warm enough for cattle. Looks were exchanged. My neighbour reckoned that it would take a fortnight of good drying weather before he would put cattle on it. A starting price was launched. Most people kept their eyes down or gazed into the distance. The auctioneer's patter accelerated and expressed growing incredulity as the price fell a stage or two and brought no response. After another drop a bid was made by means of an exchange of glances. There was no competitor. This lot, like most of them, went for around £50 per acre. The word was that when agricultural land could be bought for £1,000 per acre and interest rates were low, there were not so many who would rent it.

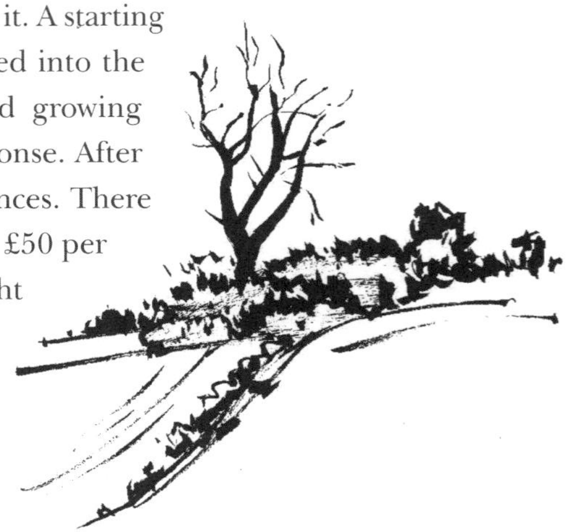

May Day

Whatever changes politicians may have in mind for May Day holidays, our village is robustly reviving ancient traditions. Leaflets advertised the 'Jack-in-the-Green Sweep's Festival'. The village's own chimney sweep was both inspiration and organiser. There was initial anxiety about the rumoured pagan origins of the event. But then an informative leaflet was produced from Rochester, where the sweeps' festival is well established. Jack-in-the green, it seems, appeared at dawn on May Day, at the climax of the rites of Beltane. He represented the spirit of the king sacrificed earlier, now reborn by the power of the sun which was represented by the 'Ban-fire'. He was a symbol of resurrection and appropriated by churches at Easter when the Jack – in a wooden framework festooned with greenery – was set up in the nave of the church as an allegorical figure. Outside the church, dancers round the Ban-fire, with sooty faces, became an important feature of the festivities. Black-faced ('Moorish' or 'Morris') dancers were then the link with the chimney sweeps, who came to be thought of as associated with the new life, and lucky at weddings. Our event was faithful to the antecedents described in the leaflet. Jack-in-the-green was authentic in his pyramid frame. We had the Dorset Triumph Morris dancers and the Treacle Eater clog dancers. The children of Templecombe primary school, in traditional dress, danced around the maypole. Entirely in the spirit of earlier festivals, though less directly significant as symbols, were the Shaftesbury Town Silver Band, lambs from Farmer Giles's Farmstead (which you could feed from a bottle), baby rabbits, and old farm machinery wheezing and puffing. You could guess the name of a lamb, or the weight of a very big, rather taciturn white goat. There were ice creams and a tea tent. Cars lined the approach roads to the tiny village, and more than 500 people had a wonderful time. It felt like a good way for Christians or people of any persuasion to celebrate new life.

Village Fund Raising

The April spirit that sent Chaucer's folk on pilgrimages seems, in our village, to have aroused a widespread fervour for fund-raising. There are projects to sustain two of its four public buildings, the church and the village hall. The others – school and inn – have their own continuous and well-tried ways of staying healthily in business. At the church's annual meeting, 19 people confidently addressed the fact that the tower was crumbling, and that the sums required to pay for repairs will, in relation to the tiny size of the congregation, be enormous. But never mind the sociological upheavals and acute shortage of clergy in the countryside, the April spirit affirmed that the tower will be saved. Meanwhile, the cricket and football clubs are thriving and badly need proper changing facilities. These can be provided by adding an extension to the village hall, which will also enhance provision for school drama, the dog-training class, the Women's Institute and the Badminton club, as well as attracting new users. So one group of people is preparing for a grand launch of the church tower appeal in September, while a quite separate group has already begun to raise money for the hall. Perhaps there was a touch of irony about starting in Wincanton's new out-of-town supermarket. People who raise money to conserve rural places and institutions might be expected to line up with the protestors against such alien things as hypermarkets. But – as funnels of icy wind were sent rifling between the sets of automatic doors each time one of the Boy Scouts moved (they were competing with a coin trail outside, to fund repairs to their hut) – we shamelessly accepted the hospitality that sheltered us and the generosity that donated the prizes. We hope the sun will shine on the trinket stall and plant sale in May, the coffee morning in June, and especially on the tombola, treasure-hunt and barbecue in July.

Molehills, Sheep, and the Heronry

The moles have been inactive for a week. No new eruptions have occurred on the lawn. A theory is that, as the top of the ground has dried out, the worms have gone deeper seeking moisture and the moles are burrowing down after them. This sounds like a more convincing explanation than our folk-remedy, which involved putting garlic and rotting fish in the entrance to the mole run. On the marsh, the Dartmoor Greyface ewes have produced 16 lambs. Several have black knees and one a black Wellington boot. Either counts as a blemish for show purposes. But three, a good proportion, look like growing to be promising prize contenders. Further afield there are interesting happenings near the town of Wedmore, once an island, where a sundial by the fine church commemorates the 800th anniversary of the Peace of Wedmore made between Alfred and Gudrun the Dane. The low ground between Wedmore and Glastonbury is a flat, marshy wilderness, divided only by a grid of watery ditches where the eels thrive, and narrow, straight causeways. It is empty except for the occasional lone tree or straggling copse. One of the copses, almost large enough to be called a wood, and surrounded by a moat, is home to a colony of herons that fish the surrounding waters. They are very active now, building nests and feeding their young. Their raucous clamour can be heard from far away. Two adult birds, showing up pale against the dark, leafless twigs of the treetops, were stationary for a long while, as if on lookout duty. Lone adults, one every few minutes, flew inwards carrying twigs or food. Others flew outwards looking for more. The traffic and noise were constant. Landing technique is impressively neat for so large a bird. The elegant sweep of the wings slows to a final glide, tiny upward hover, and precise drop beside the nest. Take-off is more awkward, as spindly legs are arthritically unfolded. If you look up through the network of black branches against the sky, you see herons darting purposefully to and fro below the canopy and somehow avoiding collision.

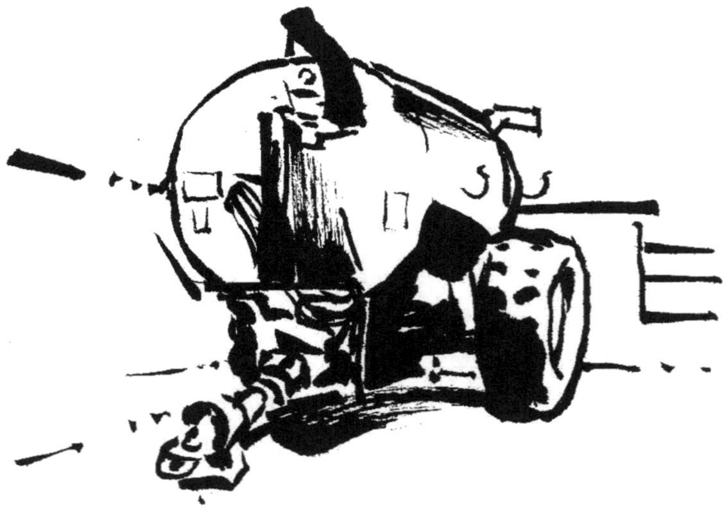

Village Hall Agenda

Regulations to guard health and safety made it necessary to explore the pipeline leading to the village hall's septic tank. Some sceptical long-time residents were confident that it ran a few yards into the squire's field and then just stopped, the tank having been a fiction. The manhole shown on the plans was not to be seen on the ground, and the cost of connecting to mains drainage was estimated at £10,000, whilst a new septic tank would cost some £3,000. Repair of the existing system (if indeed the plans proved to relate to anything that existed in fact) would probably be relatively modest. The squire, one of whose forebears gave the hall to the village in 1907, was optimistic. An exploration was authorised, and a fund-raising programme begun. At the meeting two months later, the chairman reported a highly satisfactory outcome. The pipe system had been traced to a spot in the field where the manhole had been obscured by ploughing. All necessary work, including the construction of a protective concrete dome, has been completed at a cost of £146.00. There was more good news, this time about stage curtains. A resourceful resident had access to a vast curtain formerly hung at the London Palladium. Someone had volunteered to cut it to size and re-hem it. The work has now been done, and a sophisticated system of concealed lighting installed, paid for with some of what we did not have to spend on the sewage system. The hall is now resplendent, worthy of its past (it is the place for cricket-club teas, and on the ground next door, before the turn of the century, the village played Somerset and won) and of its current valuable programme of events. Weekly bookings are for dog-training, mothers and toddlers, badminton, an upholstery class, and cricket teas in the summer. The Women's Institute takes the hall monthly. Frequent bookings are for children's and teenage parties, wedding receptions, coffee mornings, and sales. St. Margaret's Hall is a dignified and well-appointed stone building and a prime contributor to the community's life. And now it is also hygienic.

Hedges and Farming Hazards

The hedge alongside Back Lane is patchy – pale green where hawthorn is just in leaf, with darker green in other parts, splashes of white where Blackthorn has flowered, and stretches of still bare, wintry wood. We found seven kinds of woody growth, including Hornbeam, Buckthorn and Elder, in a 30-yard section. Such a frequency of types, according to the hedge-dater's rule of thumb (Hooper's Rule), suggests a venerable hedge. This one may have kept cattle in their place for hundreds of years.

Further afield, on the verge, a milk bottle shape made of wood, eight feet tall and four feet wide and painted white, bears the words: "Doorstep 71p per litre... Farmer 16p per litre... Who's milking whom?" Across a ploughed field, fixed to the outstretched, tubular arms of a giant spreader is the legend: "16 families and 40 miles of hedge to support. Please buy British." A friend who helps a dairy farmer invited me to early morning milking to see the milk hosed directly into the slurry pit. Another dairy farmer leaned over the church pew to say that he had finally given up.

The early April weather has been sharply variable. After some days when new-born lambs had been dozing in warm sunshine, we shivered on the top of Ham Hill, over 300 feet up, our eyes watering in a bitter wind. The ground there is pitted from centuries of quarrying for the golden stone that built Montacute. We could just see Creech Hill, 18 miles to the east, and Alfred's Tower, a misty outline, 28 miles in the same direction.

Round a point or two to the north there was snow on the Mendips. We heard later that one farmer above Wells had lost 100 lambs in a six foot snowdrift. Another, in an operation that involved fire brigades and volunteers, had rescued over 80, his young son reviving the almost lifeless creatures by rubbing them with straw. The market price of each lamb was only a pound or two and the impulse to save them evidently not rooted solely in commercial calculation.

Foot and Mouth

Any story concerning the local effect of foot and mouth disease is out of date as soon as written. At the school gate and the checkout, people exchange the latest word. I was told that 9am was the best time to talk to a farmer who, single-handed, keeps a dairy herd and some beef cattle.

By that time he has been up for three and a half hours, scraped the yard, fed and milked the cows nearest the farmhouse and can snatch breakfast before going two miles on the tractor to repeat the process for animals further away. He was on the telephone to Taunton. Had the suspected case at Henstridge been confirmed or cleared? His farm is within the critical 8 km radius so he cannot move stock while suspicion remains, and he needed to move eight beef animals urgently because they were almost 30 months old, after which (despite the impeccable record on their passports) they are unsaleable because of BSE regulations.

The answer was that the Henstridge case was still unproven so he could not move them. A few days later, none of the 230 cases nationally were in South Somerset. We had escaped the horrors endured elsewhere but were not unaffected. One local flock of sheep had lambed in late January. Their nursery paddock near the barn is low-lying and after heavy rainfall, waterlogged. The lambs had mud up to their bellies and some were lame but they could not be moved.

Another flock nearby was due to lamb in April on higher and drier land but an agricultural consultant had advised their owner to abandon the sheep and concentrate on holiday lets. Since then, foot and mouth has closed the countryside down and made holiday cancellations.

Hardy's Mellstock

An errand to Dorchester happened to fall on exactly the kind of fresh, bright May morning that, after the long miseries that many rural folk have suffered through winter and spring, was just what was needed to lift the spirit. Beside the road that winds through straggling, thatched villages ... Buckland Newton, Alton Pancras, Piddletrenthide ... the hedgerows were green with new growth and in patches brilliant with blackthorn in flower. The sun lit up blossom in flowering trees, and, over the hedges, the blacks, whites, browns and reds of grazing cattle and jumping lambs, pictures of health, happiness and plenty in the English countryside, the very antithesis of all those dark images of muddy pits full of twisted, smoking carcasses. We arrived in the parish that Hardy called Mellstock, five scattered hamlets with a population of around 300, centred on the ancient church where three generations of Hardys played in the string choir up in the gallery. To reduce the danger of infection in livestock, the County Agricultural College had set up thorough arrangements for disinfecting tyres and footwear at points of entry, so we could walk in the bluebell woods of Puddletown Forest. Our footpath took us over humps and hollows to the Hardy cottage which, before 20th century plantings, used to stand at the edge of a great expanse of open heathland where "the trifling irregularities were not caused by pickaxe, plough or spade, but remained as the very finger-touches of the last geological change", and where a wide, white footpath still traces some of the route of the Roman road. We were lucky enough to be there when "the May month flaps its glad green leaves".

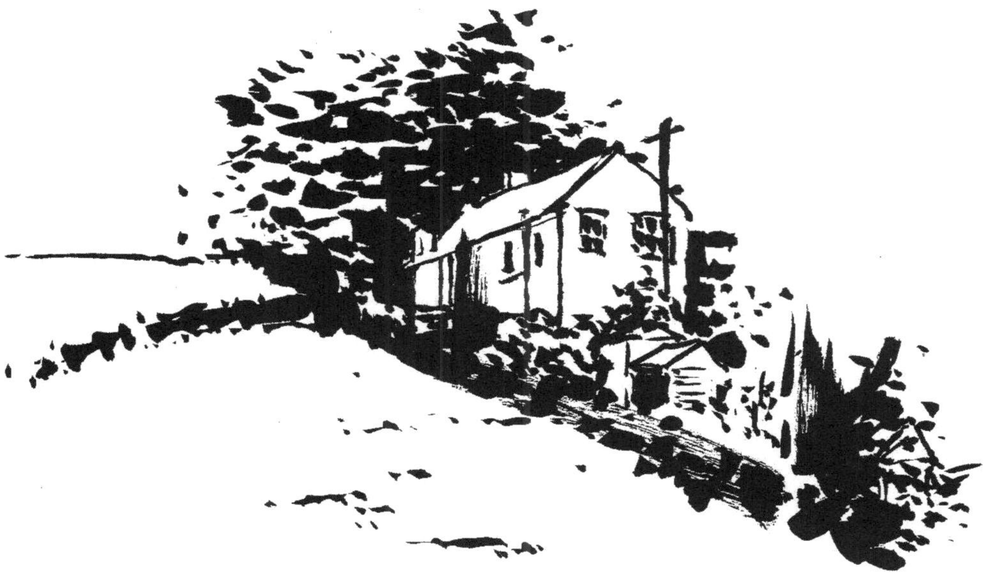

Storm Clouds at Clevedon

On the same day, you could read the headline "Gales and snowstorms batter Britain" and reports that the warmest winter for 300 years had brought spring three weeks early. While people in the North suffered power failures or were cut off by snowdrifts, we saw, on what began, admittedly, as a dark, wet and windy Saturday, plenty of signs of spring: nearby lambs already sturdily adolescent, men priming their lawnmowers, daffodils in full bloom on all sides, and the remains of emergent badgers killed by road traffic.

There was blossom on blackthorn in the hedges and on flowering cherries. Even here, though, the gusty wind was strong enough to toss the trees to and fro, and chase the dark clouds across the sky. The views at Clevedon are theatrical even in calm weather. Steep hills and valleys lead to sheer cliffs and the sea, with Wales just across the water. Surf rolls in over ribs of rock, and ornate buildings are perched on hills. With the stylish bandstand and the most elegant of piers (150 years old and recently restored, looking almost too slender and fragile to withstand wind and water) they are evidence of the development from agricultural village into polite resort that happened half way through the 19th century.

From just above the beach we had a balcony view. The sea was green and getting rougher, but there was still bright sunshine in the foreground as children bent down to collect shells and pebbles, and people walked their dogs. We watched as a dark curtain of storm-cloud and rain fell suddenly over the Welsh background and then swept in across the channel in a matter of seconds, scattering the people on the beach with pelting rain and hailstones.

Alfred's Athelney

Somerset's central lowlands, the Avalon and Sedgemoor of history and legend, have been described as a "spongy saucer"; tracts of peat and silty soil are bounded by hill ranges – Mendips, Quantocks, Blackdowns and Brendons – and by the Bristol Channel, with the coastal embankments man has laboriously made as defences against its exceptionally high tides.

Muddy, creeping rivers descend at an incline of only an inch per mile towards the sea. Man-made banks keep them from spreading except in times of flood, and elevated roadways link patches of relatively high land to which early settlers, the "Sumorsæte", and their cattle retreated for winter, while the pastures they used for summer grazing were flooded and fertilised with rich "heavy water" from the surrounding hills.

On a drizzly morning last week, the heart of this territory looked desolate, grey and featureless. We stood in a lay-by near the River Tone at Lyng and stared at an unremarkable low bank where a few sheep had settled. There was no other sign of life, nothing to enliven the view or excite the imagination.

Yet the place marks a turning point in history. Two acres of dry land here were inaccessible in 878 except by boat, defended by flood and thick beds of sedge and willow. It is where Alfred hid after defeat by the Danes, recovered himself, and gradually, from these unpromising surroundings, assembled a force to mount the decisive counterattack. Nothing survives above ground of the abbey he built on this "Isle of Athelney" in gratitude for God's deliverance and the preservation of his kingdom.

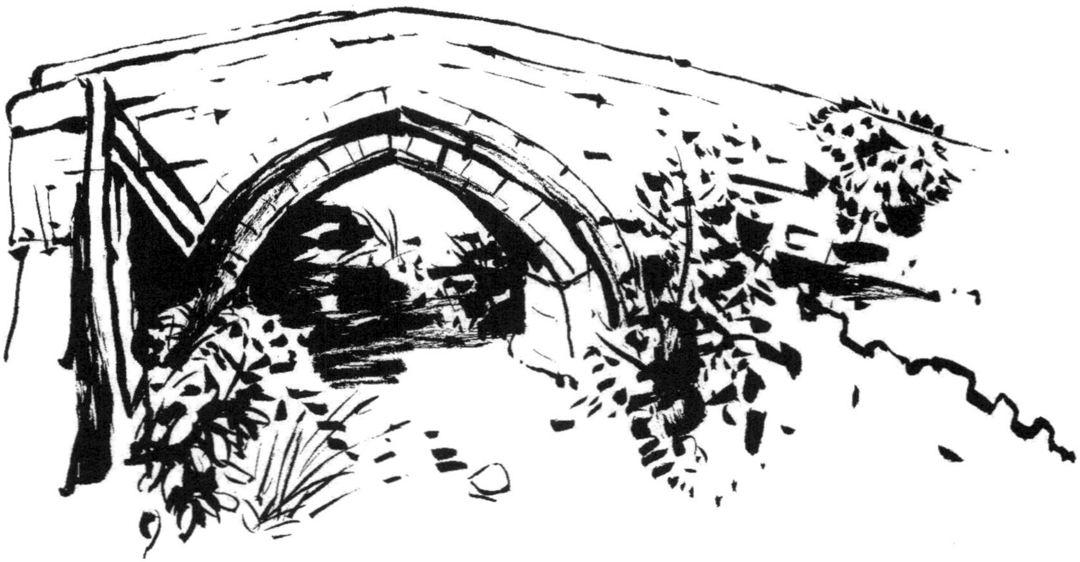

packhorse
bridge
Bruton

Powerful Currents

Living in Bruton, we used to regard the River Brue as a tame little stream, hardly a source of power, except once every few years when it would surprise us by flooding violently, overwhelming the bridges and sending metal dustbins rattling down the lane. But the other day I went to Gant's Mill, a little way downstream from the town, and saw the foaming cascade at the overflow – where excess water not needed to drive the turbines crashes down into a pool to be fed back into the river. It demonstrated what a powerful resource the modest river in fact represents.

The Brue's flow has been sufficiently strong and reliable across the years since 1290, when John of Gaunt first built a fulling mill here, to operate wheel or turbine more or less continuously. The first turbine replaced the waterwheel in 1888, when the mill was grinding corn, and it still works today, grinding corn to feed the sheep that graze the riverside pasture. But now a new kind of cross-flow turbine has been developed, which converts the Brue's power into electricity.

The District Council and 12 South Somerset mill-owners co-operated to set up a hydro-power project; together the mills will make enough electricity to power 150 homes; to generate as much by burning fossil fuels would create 260 tonnes of carbon dioxide emissions. We live beside a millpond, and the old, overshot waterwheel rusts unused next-door. The streams that flow through this landscape of hills and valleys have, until quite recent times, been the prime local source of power. Now technology has been devised to exploit their power again, and without any harm to the environment of which they are a vital part.

Wessex Ridgeway

Through much of the heart of Dorset, there are great, rolling chalk hills, and the roads and flinty tracks that keep to the high ground and run along the ridges offer spacious views in all directions, back to Blackmore Vale, down towards the sea, and across the vast tract of Cranborne Chase. The villages lie mostly along the roads in the narrow river valleys, but we came to one up on the heights – Ashmore, the highest village in the county – when we were looking for the first Dorset section of the Wessex Ridgeway. The Ramblers' Association established this route, to follow parts of the ancient Great Ridgeway and run down to the coast at Lyme Regis. The eight or nine steep hairpin bends of Zig Zag hill, near Shaftesbury, brought us up close to the village at 700 ft.

Once there, we might well have lingered, because Ashmore is almost too picturesque to be true. There is a round village pond, with ducks and a cedar tree, and a harmonious range of buildings in flint, stone and brick. But we set our face towards the bridleway, past an orchard carpeted with snowdrops, and paused at a field-gate for the view that, on a clear day, reaches down to the Isle of Wight. There were lingering patches of snow, and plump, frisky adolescent lambs beside our track. After a mile or so, a solitary rider came past. Then a jogger with a terrier crossed our path and startled a fawn, which performed a superb deer-leap and, in a few more elegant bounds, left the Jack Russell panting hopelessly behind and disappeared into a copse. Then our own footsteps disturbed a hare, which careered crazily away to be lost in the stubble. As we turned back towards the village there was a cutting wind in our faces, but the sun was beginning to shine, and the scene when we reached the pond was even more engaging than when we had left it.

Churches on The Levels

We had been away and after the long, dry and often cold spring, the countryside had changed markedly in the week since we had last seen it. They call a cold winter a "blackthorn winter", and this past one surely qualifies, for white blackthorn was flowering in extraordinary profusion on hedges now more green than black. Our way was through watery lowlands beside the pollarded willows that line the streams. Great perpendicular church towers stand up from the flats, and we passed close by one of the best, miraculous in its tracery and delicate pinnacles, at Huish Episcopi. Then it was on to Curry Rivel where we turned aside from the rows of houses to take a little lane into another world, the seclusion of Manor Green – thatched cottages, Manor Farm and St. Andrew's church, where the organ was playing, and flower-arrangers were decking out nave and aisles for the wedding of the organist's daughter. As we went on along the ridge towards Swell, the view to the north was across West Sedgemoor, towards the Parrett estuary where it widens out into Bridgwater Bay. Another narrow lane took us down to Swell Court, a wonderful 15th century manor with yew trees, lines of poplar and a heronry nearby. There was no sound from the empty yards and barns, and you might have expected the little church that stands beside the house to be closed or even derelict, but its cherry tree was in blossom and its door invitingly open. And it was vigorously alive in the hands of the present rector. The first one listed on the board took office in 1319.

Duncliffe

On the day we planned to visit Duncliffe Wood, near Shaftesbury, a spokesman for the Woodland Trust told the BBC that, across the country, 360 woodlands were threatened by development programmes, whether for roads, buildings, airports or golf-courses. But Duncliffe Wood, bought by the Woodland Trust in 1984, looks safe. Its 86 hectares are spread over the twin summits of Duncliffe Hill, a landmark prominently visible from miles around, standing up to a height of 210 metres from the valleys and once marshy flats of Blackmoor Vale. The hill is too steep for runways, fairways or housing estates, an unlikely route for a motorway, and too far out of town for a retail park. In the 1950s and 1960s the threat to Duncliffe's traditional character as an ancient woodland of oak, ash, hazel and lime was a programme of felling native broadleaf trees to make way for the commercial planting of conifers. The trust has reversed this process and, as we walked along the entrance bridleway (with the rattle of a woodpecker echoing from our left) and looked ahead, we saw mainly the varied greens of spring growth in broadleaf trees, with, towards the top, a few dark spears of conifer. Then the eye was attracted by a vivid flash of blue-violet, lower down – the first patch of bluebells at the fringe of the wood. Inside, the flowers covered whole sweeps of the wood's bed. Thomas Hardy identified trees with his eyes shut by listening to the wind among the leaves, but we needed a leaflet to plot our way to a circle of small-leafed lime, said to be 600 years old – the oldest living things in Dorset. Through a gate, a field dotted with sheep sloped down to the vale. The view beyond was north-west, towards Stourhead, but the haze meant that we could not make out the silhouette of Alfred's tower.

West Country Waterways

Somerset rivers tend to meander indecisively for much of their length across the flat central lowlands. The Brue is already below high-tide level when it reaches Godney Moor, and a long stretch of the Parrett falls at only one foot per mile. We encountered a very different terrain and a different kind of river when we took a detour through rural Shropshire close to Telford, named after the maker of canals, bridges and viaducts, one of the men who, in the 18th century, worked on the natural resources of this landscape of steep, wooded hills and made it the cradle of the Industrial Revolution.

The Severn has already curled through Wales, passed Shrewsbury and become a substantial waterway by the time it reaches this stretch near Coalport. Coal had long been exported to Gloucester on barges that returned with cider and hay. The gorge where we walked has recovered much of its rustic quiet, but is close to where Abraham Darby, a Quaker manufacturer, first produced iron in a coke-fired furnace, and started a thriving industry. His grandson, Abraham Darby III, built the cast-iron bridge we stood and marvelled at, the first in the world, with a great semi-circular arch. It was opened in 1781.

Below Gloucester, the Severn widens towards the Bristol Channel, and way downstream the Parrett crawls out through the slime of its own flat estuary to join it. The Gloucestershire Avon emerges from between the sheer, 240 ft walls of the Clifton gorge, a setting dramatic enough to inspire Brunel to devise a suspension bridge whose daring and elegance still take the breath away. Back in Somerset we were in our familiar world of stone bridges and humbler crossings for man and beast over streams that drain the pasture.

Hedge-laying Skills

The road between Wincanton and Sherborne passes between a variety of banks and hedges that divide it from fields on both sides which are mostly grazed by sheep. Some of the hedges have been trimmed into more or less uniform shapes by mechanical cutters; some are healthy, thick and impenetrable, but others are neglected, with straggling growth at the top, and meagre, gappy bases that an enterprising lamb would get through without difficulty. So it has been good to see three men, a father and two sons, working on two lengths of hedge with the traditional bill-hook, carrying out what was once one of every farmer's winter chores, that of hedge-laying.

Hedge-laying encourages new growth at the base of the hedge to make a windproof barrier, and one of the sons told me that it gives small birds some protection at the top against sparrowhawks. I had caught up with him in a barn, when he was inspecting a heavily pregnant pedigree Suffolk ewe. He told me that the skill of hedge-laying had been passed down in his family. The key technique involves making slanting cuts through the stout uprights so that they can be gently bent down almost to the horizontal, without snapping, to form the "pleachers", close enough together to form a firm structure, but wide enough apart to leave space for new growth. I went the next day to look at the result of the work. Hedges are traditionally measured in "chains". He said they had done 11 (some 200 metres) in five days. The thickest uprights had been cut with a chainsaw. The pleachers were hazel poles as thick as your arm and up to three metres long, and the top of the hedge was a rounded mat of brushwood securely bound in with hoops of bent hazel. It will be interesting to watch this hedge's development with each new growth.

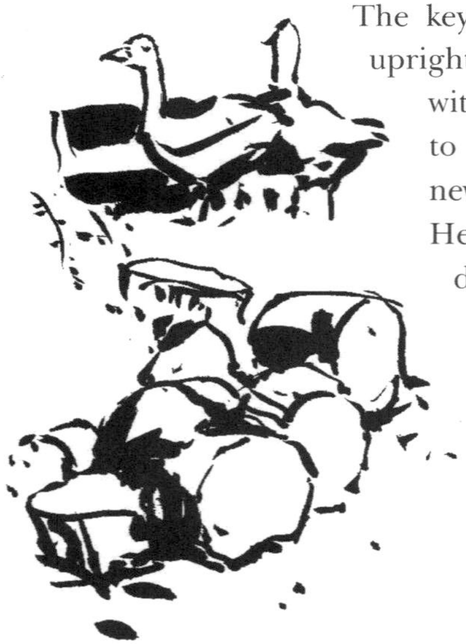

Dorset Winterbornes

The seasonal streams that are fed by springs in the underlying chalk near Dorchester have led to the inclusion of the word winterborne in the names of 15 Dorset villages. In summer long stretches of these streams can run dry, but when rain comes it recharges the underground aquifers so that water seeps up to replenish them. We saw one of the streams, the South Winterborne, gurgling through roadside gullies at Winterborne Abbas, near its source, then apparently running dry across a field downstream, but then reviving further along its course where water welled up through the grass to make a wide pool. The South Winterborne first rises from a spring above Winterborne Abbas, then runs down through Winterborne St. Martin to join the Dorset Frome at West Stafford. Some of the Winterborne villages, such as Winterborne Abbas, evidently prosper, but others have become quiet backwaters. At Winterborne Came a broad sweep of open land slopes gently up from the riverbed towards a copse and the perfectly proportioned classical facade of Came House. The village nowadays consists simply of the great house, with its various satellite buildings and outhouses, and downhill, beyond another quiet patch of woodland, the walled kitchen garden and ancient church. A leaflet inside the church tells of a string of agricultural settlements along the South Winterborne valley depleted or abandoned through the 15th and 16th centuries, as large-scale sheep farming took over the land. Came church survived to serve the people of the mansion and its estate. From 1862 to his death in 1886, the vicar was William Barnes, a venerated scholar, poet and priest, honoured with a statue in Dorchester. A little way further on, we searched beside the stream for the remains of Winterborne Farringdon, but could find nothing of this settlement but grassy humps and hollows to hint at what once was there.

Thoroughbred Foal

The village's name is said to mean "the settlement of the horse-keepers", and it remains remarkably apt. There are three ponies and a pony-trap next door, the dressage training establishment is a few fields further on, and around the corner is the stud where thoroughbred mares are at this time of year giving birth to foals destined for the racetrack.

I was there one morning recently and taken to the "foaling box" to see a foal that had been born in the night. Ignorant of horses and their ways, I was astonished to see such a confident young animal only a few hours old already standing tall on her long legs – almost half as tall as her mother – and eagerly exploring her new world.

A few days later I saw a second foal, this one a colt and two days old, being led out into the paddock with his mother. When the door opened he butted me familiarly in the chest, sniffed the air and quivered with the thrill of heading for the great outside. Given half a chance, he would have darted off on his own. The moment he was released in the paddock, he did take off, accelerating away at astonishing speed, wheeling around a tight curve like a champion and kicking his heels in the air.

Horses, I was told, are flight animals, creatures that need to be able to run fast in the wild, particularly when newborn and at their most vulnerable to predators. Characteristics that might one day lead this colt to the winner's enclosure derive from his primitive ancestry.

Mares almost always give birth at night when darkness would have offered wild horses some cover. By morning, as I had seen, a foal is no longer a sitting target. Two spirited yearlings in a larger paddock galloped over to meet us at the gate and nibbled at our coat collars. Their own winter coats were rough and woolly. Soon they will go to the sales at Newmarket or Deauville.

Gurnard's Head

We had often, on annual trips to the far end of Cornwall, passed the Gurnard's Head Inn, which stands at a corner on the way to St. Ives, but we had never gone down the path to the headland from which it takes its name. The path starts between grey coastguard cottages and farm buildings and passes through granite stiles. In the first field, a cow was bellowing mournfully, its thin and sickly looking calf huddled down against the wall, while the rest of the suckling herd, adult and young, galloped cheerfully away to fresh pastures. Where the track divides, we took the right hand way, and when we had gone a little downhill, saw the headland, slightly indistinct in the mist, across a little inlet to our left.

In the foreground, beside Treen Cove, was a ruined tower, a remnant of the engine house of Treen copper mine. We stood beside it and took in the view of the promontory jutting defiantly into the ocean. The mist was lifting, and it took little imagination to relate the jagged, rocky outline to the look of a gurnard's large, bony head on the fishmonger's slab. Francis Kilvert visited this spot in 1870 and wrote in his diary: "I wandered round the cliffs to the broken rocks at the furthest point on the head, and sat alone among the wilderness of broken, shattered tumbled cliffs, listening to the booming and breaking of the waves below, and watching the flying skirts of the showers of spray. Perfect solitude." Solitude was not, for us, perfect; but we were happy to meet another walker who told us that Aldous Huxley, as a boy brought here by his father, simply stood, stared and said, less poetically than Kilvert: "Bloody marvellous!" The ramparts and ditches, remains of an ancient, fortified castle and the surviving evidence of 16 prehistoric roundhouses and a chapel, seem appropriate to the awe-inspiring character of the place. Gurnard's Head has also, unsurprisingly, been used as a look-out post for spotting shoals of pilchard.

Quiet Corner Farm

The name Quiet Corner Farm is recorded on 1839 tithe maps of Henstridge and still survives today. In the village magazine, the news from Quiet Corner refers to the success of the community apple juicing project in 2008 and promises a repeat next September. And it calls attention to the admirable work of a one-time champion hedge layer whose traditional handiwork may be admired along Oak Vale Lane outside the farm. So I went down to Henstridge, turned into Blackmoor Road, which runs downhill from the ridge of the village's name towards the low-lying vale, and went round to the farm entrance, noting the finely managed hedge as I passed. Through the field gate, I dodged the bantam hens, went up the drive between two orchards, and came to a group of buildings – an original threshing barn, work-horse stable and open-fronted cart-shed – all now converted into inviting living spaces and grouped around what used to be the bullock yard.

The farm's previous owners, three brothers and a sister, used to take apples by train to Sturminster market when Henstridge had a station on the Somerset & Dorset railway line. But station, railway and market are long gone. The present owners, new to the business and the district, started by taking apples to farmers markets and a local cider-maker. Recently, the Healthy Living Centre in Wincanton has involved the farm in the community juicing project and provided a press. Last season's output was 1,000 bottles of juice, all done by hand. And now there is a new mechanical crusher, as yet unpacked. We looked at apple trees, some new saplings and some wizened ancients, among them Newton Wonders, Annie Elizabeths, Old Somerset Russets, and a medieval apple called the French Crab that you can still pick in February. There were plum trees and a Golden Drop greengage. Wandering the orchards were three resident Shetland ponies: a four-year-old mare awaiting her first foal, a 20-year-old stallion and a young colt. Their firm, broad backs suggest the compact power that once equipped Shetlands to be pit ponies.

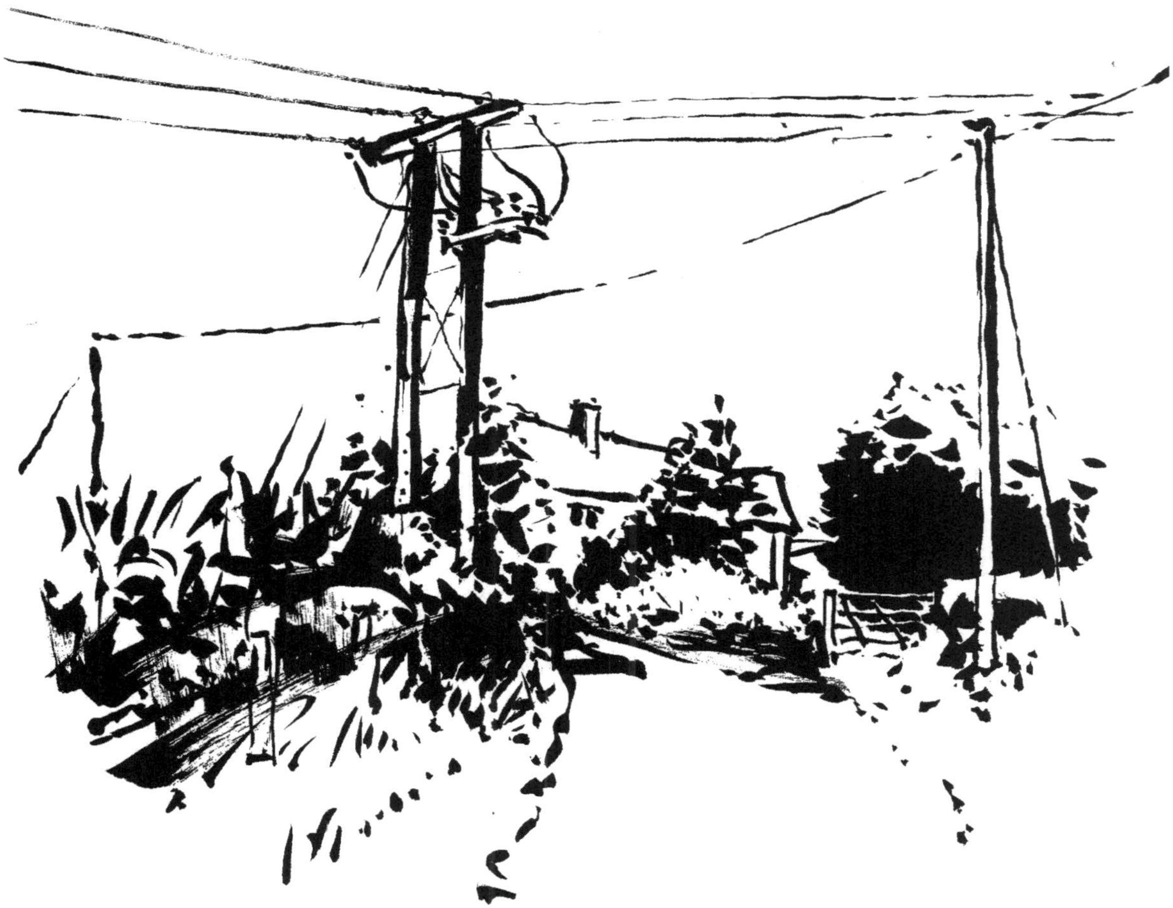

Yarlington Fringe

A long time ago, I heard that a notable Somerset cider apple, the Yarlington Mill – pear-shaped, russet skinned and medium bitter-sweet – originated when a pip found its way by chance into a crevice in the stonework of the watermill at Yarlington, and took root. Most travellers between Wincanton and Shepton Mallet are unaware that they are passing close by the village of Yarlington, screened by trees down in its shadowy hollow. But when a phone call summoned us to the Yarlington Fringe Festival, I remembered the cider apple, and wondered if I might find the old stone wall where it was born.

We threaded our way down the narrow lane, between wandering groups of adults, face-painted children and dogs, then through the throng in the open space between pub and church to the crowded car park on a sloping field. It seemed as if all Somerset had found its way to this small, secluded place. I spotted someone who, I was sure, would know about the apple, but was told that, though there was still a mill farm, there was now no mill.

But there was plenty of evidence of cider's enduring popularity in the convivial groups outside the Stag's Head, where people were gathering for the next performance in the acoustic tent. Behind the tent, a man was studiously tuning a beautifully fashioned and unfamiliar stringed instrument on the churchyard wall. He told me it was a modern dulcimer made in Glastonbury. Next, we looked into the church, where the opera workshop was advertised. Enthusiasts were being put through their movements for the opening scene of Tosca. Back outside, an expert in survival techniques was demonstrating how to build your own pizza oven from clay, sand and straw. We had missed the duck race, the basket-weaving workshop, the jazz quartet and the Langport Mummers, but on the way uphill, out of the village, looked into what must be one of the smallest village halls in England to admire the work of 25 local artists.

Hydraulic Ram

High up at Winyard's Gap, southeast of Crewkerne, the switchback road winds between the beech woods and round the shoulders of steep hillsides, opening up a bewildering succession of dramatic views, one moment eastwards into Dorset and the next northwest into Somerset. There are plentiful water springs, and pools where water has gathered on the hillside shelves and terraces. The rivers Parrett and Axe rise here, the Parrett to wander across the Somerset Levels and up to the Severn estuary, and the Axe to flow down to Lyme Bay.

We had gone to see the ingenious device whereby a farmer lifts water about 200ft from a spring to a reservoir, which holds 11,000 gallons and serves the animals of two farms and the human tenants in 11 properties, without recourse to any power other than that of the water itself and gravity. We were taken first to the hilltop, where a ball's position at the top of a pole signified that the reservoir was full to the brim. Next, we clambered down beside a big house, once derelict (water sometimes used to seep up through the floor) but now splendidly renovated.

In the rough grass on the hillside, we saw the spot where the spring delivered a steady flow to a pipe that ran down to the header tank, building up a sufficient head to operate the hydraulic ram, which, since 1947, with very little in the way of maintenance or repair, has steadily thumped away and done its remarkable job. And there is more hydraulic power to spare; an overflow pipe runs down to another header tank for a second ram. When the manhole was lifted, there was little to see but the round top of a modestly sized cylinder. But as we looked up the sheer face of the ridge towards the reservoir, the effective power of this unassuming piece of machinery was hard to credit.

Changing Ways at Batcombe

Guidebooks rightly praise the views from Batcombe churchyard. Sir Nikolaus Pevsner in his guide to North Somerset and Bristol writes: "Fine view, with, in the foreground, a sycamore planted in 1750," and "Nearly as fine, the view from the W with the tower behind a cedar tree."

When a history of Batcombe by Captain GT Coney OBE RN, kindly sent to me by a Country Diary reader, drew me back to that churchyard, the views across valleys and heights lived up to expectation; to the south, broken cloud and a blue sky made a shifting pattern of light and shade on the steeply sloping planes of the hillsides.

Coney's book gives some remarkable nuggets of information. Between 1910 and 1914, for example, the postman walked from Evercreech to Upton Noble, some five miles, with the mail, and spent the day in a hut there, where he cut hair for threepence and gave violin lessons before walking the afternoon mail back to Evercreech. We read that the Rev Thomas Coney, clerk, was one of the founders of the village school (1826) whose neatly symmetrical building, now a village hall, still stands at the edge of the churchyard. The trustees laid down uncompromising conditions of employment for the master and mistress; they were to be members of the Church of England, of sober life and conversation, and frequenters of the Holy Communion, and were to bring the children to church on Sunday.

Late in the 19th century there were no fewer than seven railway stations within five miles of the village, and good connections by horse and cart. It was possible to have fish from Hull or Grimsby in the house less than 24 hours after dispatch from the quayside. The altered disposition of 100 village dwellings between 1938 and the late 1950s indicates typical mid-century changes in village life. By the later date, 15 workers' cottages had become holiday homes as against only two before the war, and 23 families (as against only four) had come to Batcombe to retire.

Coker History

After a spell away, it was a very English experience to walk past thatched cottages on the fringe of a Somerset village and feel the keen, February wind when it gusted. In North Coker, across the stream from Eliot's East Coker, and past an orchard of bent and wizened apple-trees, there are plenty of footpaths, well signed, sometimes sheltered, and now and then opening onto surprises. The village lies on relatively low ground bordered by broad, sloping fields that would once, in season, have been blue with flax; the Coker villages were notable producers of rope and cloth. One path went between high stone walls, and another was sheltered by a wall on one side and a bank on the other with scratched mounds of sandy spoil left by badger diggings. But past the old mill, we were facing the wind again and crossing open fields. Over a stile, the next enclosed path took us to an opening into the grounds of a mansion – orchard, and walled kitchen-garden, with glasshouse – all wearing a slightly forlorn look, as if remembering more prosperous times. At the end of another enclosed lane, we came upon a neat weather- boarded chapel such as you might expect in New England, with fresh white paint and evidence of lively use. Then, a few steps away, in an unfrequented spot beside the track, Naish Priory, with fan tracery, an oriel window, octagonal chimneys, and an exquisite pointed arch. At the edge of East Coker, we peered in at the half-hidden house, long, low and thatched, where William Dampier was born in 1651. His memorial describes him as 'Buccaneer, Explorer, Hydrographer' and records that 'thrice he circumnavigated the globe, and, first of all Englishmen, explored and described the coast of Australia'.

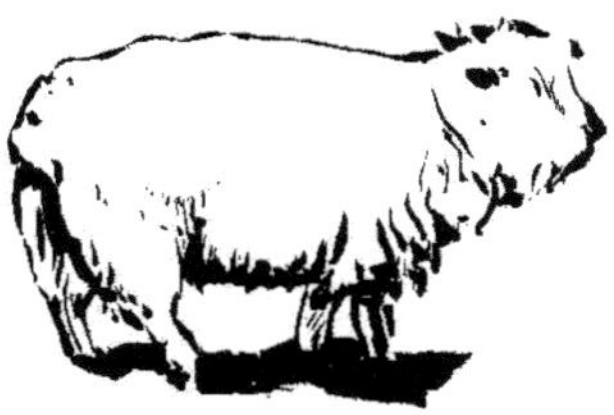

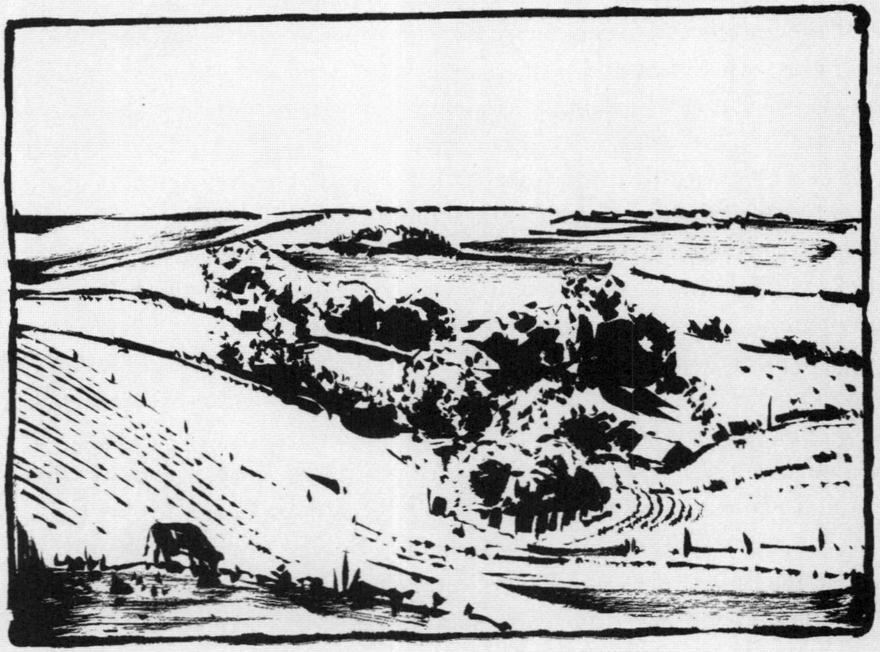

SUMMER

Prize Cattle

We are nicely placed between the vales of Camelot and Blackmoor, in rich dairy country. Farm-gate sales of milk, cream and butter are a special advantage. We approached one warmly recommended farm (two dwellings, one a listed building, with barns and milking-parlours assembled round a sizeable yard) by way of a path beside a field of grazing Jersey cows. Inquisitive, sloe-eyed calves peered out from a barn. The produce was in an unattended fridge, with a price-list beside it. You simply took your butter, cream and eggs and left the money. The cream in the Jersey milk reached almost a third of the way down the bottle. The farmer told me that he and his wife had bought this farm in 1976, when it was more or less run down and they needed to move up from their much smaller property in a neighbouring village. They now have over 250 cows mainly Jerseys. The farm, worked by husband, wife, and three sons, covers 340 acres, a few of which are down to cereals. The Jerseys are the speciality. They win prizes and appear on television. Some were sold to a princess from Bahrain, who built them air-conditioned quarters and invited the farmer and his wife to go and see how they were thriving. One of the champion cows, Polyanna, has this week successfully defended her title of Supreme Champion at the New Forest show. And those Bambi like calves are delicately bred. The family have travelled to Denmark, the USA and Canada, collecting worldwide expertise on the genetics of Jersey cattle. One of the sons goes to New Zealand later in the year to pursue the quest. So the produce in the fridge is the result of a very fine pedigree, which was recognised by the Jersey Cattle Society some years ago when they recommended cows from this farm to Anchor butter for an advertising campaign. Ten selected Jerseys went to Cricket St. Thomas for six weeks' work with an American trainer. They are the ones that kick the football on TV.

The Pig-handling Parson

There was little evidence of gloom as Somerset's agricultural community set out its stall at the Bath and West Show. Beyond the glistening Porsches, Range-Rovers and space-age farm machinery, and the tents full of waxed coats, saddlery and jodhpurs, were the Dartmoor pony class, the cheese pavilion, the shepherds' flockmasters and the parade of goats. The great champion Charolais bulls, combed and cosseted, sprawled, untroubled by CAP regulations, on beds of clean straw. There were pigs of immense size, superior beasts and stars of the show circuit, yawning at the boredom of it all. But it was the pig-handlers' competition ("one man and his pig") that specially caught the eye. Each man, armed with a wooden shield in his left hand and a short batten or crook in his right, attempted to guide his pig through a slalom of stakes and a fabric tunnel, over a ramp and a jump, into a pen, and then along the finishing straight. There was a Hickstead-style commentary and time-faults were awarded. One handler, identified as Simon, almost straddled his pig, shielding its vision from distraction on the left and nudging its rear and right side with the crook. "You don't argue with Simon" said the commentator. Most of the handlers adopted the cautious tactic of crawling through the tunnel behind the pig, but one sent his pig in and strolled alongside. His over-confidence was penalised when the pig contrived to turn in the restricted space and emerge at the start end to loud applause. The NFU and our MEP were holding conferences and serious business was being done, but the general impression was of something like an old-fashioned Derby Day. The commentator revealed that the pig-handler was "the Reverend Simon". A pig-handling West Country parson seemed just right alongside the whirring sheep-shearers and clanging blacksmiths.

Hedgehog

"The beasts are by their dens exprest," wrote Andrew Marvell, and went on to illustrate the point; "The low-roof'd tortoises do dwell / In cases fit of tortoise-shell." I wonder if he had seen a "den" like the one a friend showed me last week beside a bath in his garden. It was a neat and compact structure, some 30 inches long, 22 inches wide and 10 inches high, made of precisely-formed, horizontal layers of dry leaves and bark mulch. One side reached under the cover of a broad-leaved pulmonaria. Construction work had been speedy as well as skilful and meticulous. The owners of the house wondered what kind of creature had moved in. Wasps or hornets perhaps? The pest officer was equally baffled and conducted cautious research with a walking stick inserted through the roof. It revealed the spines on a hedgehog's back. A close watch was kept, lamps and camera poised (hedgehogs give birth in July and August). Ten days later, there was at dusk, a mighty heaving and rustling but nothing more was seen. A tray of cat-food was set beside the nest at night and the cat kept in. The food had gone each morning and no cats or other animals had been seen. Nor was anything more observed until August 20, when the cat-food was put out earlier than before and, at dusk, an unaccompanied small hedgehog crept out, ate a modest portion of the food, ignored a camera flash and returned. In the morning, the rest of the food was, as usual, gone. If Marvell was right about the significance of a beast's "denn" this one shows the hedgehog to be prudent, discreet, ingenious, and economical as well as a very fast worker.

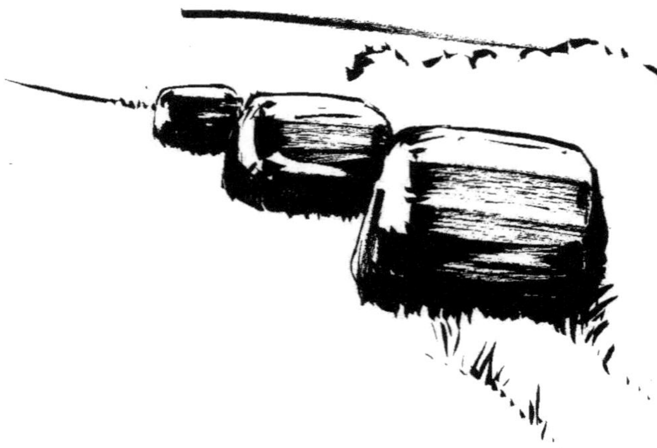

Change at the Farm

Across the cattle-grid, along the track, across empty pastureland and past the substantial, four-square farmhouse, I sat in a dark cider-barn (still functional) and heard how the owner had lived on this farm for 61 years. His grandfather, a carter, died young of pneumonia, and the widow was given a shilling a week by the parish. His father blacked boots at the rectory one day a week in return for breakfast, left school at 13 to work on the land, and often enjoyed a trussed and cooked blackbird for his packed lunch. In time, he went to the war, and afterwards demonstrated his acquired countryman's skills and instinct for good husbandry sufficiently to be granted the tenancy of a small county council holding for ex-servicemen. In 1937, now with a young family – including Bertie, my informant – he heard that a larger, privately-owned farm nearby was to let. He cycled to Castle Cary and impressed the agent as a sound man to recommend to the owner, who offered a fair deal. So the family stepped up to Higher Farm, 140 acres, 35 cows, and a steady living to be made by their co-operative effort with one horse to do the mowing, harrowing and carting and provide family transport on occasion. She would trot at a steady 13mph to Castle Cary. One, or sometimes two, men were employed. The only paperwork involved cheque-book and paying-in book and the only representative of officialdom was the local policeman. Everything was done by hand – milking, pulling weeds, making hay, building sheaves and roofing ricks. The second war brought men with maps to decree that certain fields of choice pasture be ploughed for wheat. This was more than the horse could do. The ministry supplied an iron-wheeled tractor. Mechanisation, intensification, specialisation, quotas and regulation followed. Now there are no cows and the pasture is let for "grasskeep" at falling prices.

Glastonbury

The summer solstice brings a variety of stirrings to the fields, lanes, monuments and ancient earthworks of the south-west. It was sad to hear of paint daubed on some of the stones of the Avebury circle but good to know that access to Stonehenge was granted to people who wanted to be there for the magic of the midsummer sunrise. Nearer home, groups of folk, some straggling on foot with bundles on their shoulders, and some in psychedelic minibuses, are heading across the land that was once sea or marsh towards the county's most striking landmark and potent symbol at Glastonbury Tor. There were early comers to the rock festival at Pilton, but Glastonbury, still a kind of island standing up from The Levels, draws new age pilgrims in its own right with its blend of topography, history and legend. Forty years ago, my mother, when she saw the "holy thorn", bought a booklet, and was from that point convinced that Joseph of Arimathea came here, perhaps with the young Jesus, and the magic, helpfully prompted by monks, mystics and creative thinkers, has grown over the centuries. In 1191, the monks claimed to have discovered the remains of Arthur and Guinevere, reinterred them in stately tombs, and developed the idea of Glastonbury as the ancient Avalon. We were not bent on pilgrimage, but attracted by another midsummer event organised by the solar energy society – a "celebration of renewable energy and the power of the sun which occurs annually on or around the summer solstice". Before we could find the demonstration of solar power, we were distracted by publicity surrounding the fine tower of St. John's Church. Residents have assembled opposition to the mounting of mobile phone transmitters on the church tower. Their magazine refers to the "15th century microwave transmission tower" as one of the finest examples of Somerset stonemason's craft and that "careful study of the building will reveal traces of its secondary use as a Christian church". There is serious information too, to inform a considered modern disentanglement of Glastonbury fact and myth.

Travellers

Across the marsh the road makes a gentle curve to the left. On the inside of the curve is a wide, grassy space. It is a peaceful place – the road is quiet and there are no buildings nearby. Since the Glastonbury festival, a small settlement has formed there: a single-decker bus and two trailers, one with awning extension.

A large Rottweiler chained to a stake by the bus made a violent commotion at my approach and set off the German shepherd by the nearer trailer and one or two puppies. But when I was ushered in by the bus owner, Cleo, the Rottweiler, was as warmly welcoming as her master. She has to be chained because she recently chased some sheep, and the police warned that a repetition would render her liable to be shot. But the chaining makes her more than normally fierce and territorial. Her nature changes again the moment she is released.

There are three couples in the settlement. One couple, with their two children, left Bournemouth recently. They are looking to settle. One of their children is already enrolled in the village school, and the father has a job at the chicken farm.

The other couples like the travelling life, and, looking round the site and the comfortably appointed inside of the bus, I could see the attraction. They take casual labour when they can get it or when the need (for food or gas bottles) is desperate, and avoid the complication of "signing on" if they can.

They recognise that they are not entitled to council services that others pay for but hope someone may stretch a point to allow the school bus to pause on its way past (saving a small pupil a very long walk) and that the refuse collectors may help too.

They gratefully value the help of the nearby householder who supplies water, and set that against the taunts and hooting horns of passing youngsters. No eviction order has been served, but in any case the bus-owner has itchy feet.

The Coker Villages

We found the little hamlet of Hardington Moor and asked the way to a special hay-meadow. "You're too late for the flowers", they told us. "The meadow was mown a few weeks back." But they showed us how to find it, high up on a ridge at Coker Hill. We took in the long views, north and south.

An English Nature notice explained that our meadow, on the southern flank, was one of very few examples of the traditional, unimproved grassland of which only a tiny proportion survived the post-war intensification of agriculture. It is home to the rare oat grass and green-winged orchid and is mown in July after most of the wild flowers have seeded.

When we arrived, the cows were munching grass speckled yellow with nothing rarer than dandelions. Cattle keep down the tougher grasses and allow rarer plants to thrive in season. Looking down into the valley, we saw West Coker immediately below us, a labyrinth of narrow lanes threading between ancient stone buildings. The right-angled pattern of the 16th century manor house stood out. Travellers who pass through the village by the overcrowded funnel of the old A30 gain no impression of the place's shape or character, but once you have looked down on its intricate plan spread out like a map, you want to explore.

We followed a steep track cut deep in the sandy hillside down into the village. Off Dibbles Lane were the schoolhouse and the old dairyhouse. The lanes were empty and silent until we turned a corner towards the manor house and heard cheerful sounds. Cream teas were being served in a cottage garden in aid of the Women's Institute.

People know about nearby East Coker because TS Eliot found his ancestors' birthplace there and wrote about it. Of West Coker, some may have read that it was the home of Coker canvas, prized by seafarers when hemp and flax were local products. Our good fortune was to hear its story direct from people who live there, sitting in a garden overshadowed by the manor, enjoying home-made cream teas.

New Values at the Tip

As school outings go, a day at the dump sounds unpromising, but I expect the 90 children from our village school to come back from Dimmer Tip next week with shining eyes. The tip is a patch of land outside Castle Cary, once an ammunition dump, now a landfill site, where a pond which used to be home to a community of newts is now buried 15 metres deep beneath layers of industrial and domestic waste. Shared concern for the impending fate of these newts led to a creative partnership between Wyvern Waste Services and local environmentalists. Moving the newts to a circular brick-built pool originally made for the disposal of incendiary bombs was the start of a visionary project whereby acres of rotting waste become the basis for new growth. The work is financed by the landfill tax that we pay for rubbish disposal, together with direct funding from the Wyvern company. Much of it is possible only because this site is on impermeable blue lias clay, by which any potentially harmful substance is sealed away to a standard well beyond what the regulations require. In the new visitor centre children can see how the reed-bed filtration works, how machinery is creating electricity out of the methane gas from decomposing rubbish, and watch the wind pump turn in the breeze. As they sit in a circle in the thatched Bronze Age dwelling, they will catch the enthusiasm for the badger sett, the bird-feeding station, wildflower and butterfly meadows and maybe guess at much more than the Carymoor Environmental Centre demonstrates about what to value and what to throw away.

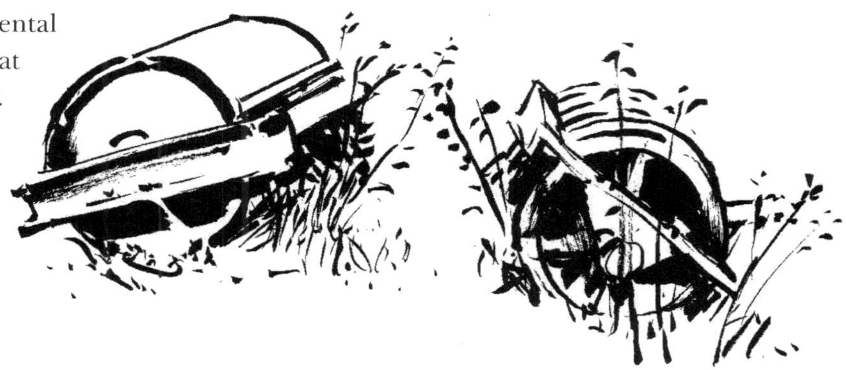

Smoked Eel

Several wandering waterways drain the moors of central Somerset. At a farm just outside Hambridge we watched a man smoking eel and saw the delight he took in his work.

The mystery whereby larvae drift on the Gulf Stream for years to arrive as tiny elvers in these Somerset rivers, mature over a decade or more and then, at the appropriate season, set out as full-grown eels on the return journey to the Sargasso Sea, produces a succulent flesh prized today as it was by medieval clergy. One fishing station alone supplied Glastonbury Abbey with 2,000 eels in a year, and in 1379, the chapter of Wells Cathedral threatened poachers with excommunication.

Today's eels are caught in an ingenious system of racks devised by the monks when the great religious houses controlled this region. Racks were set up near mills where the level and flow of the water could be controlled in relation to the depth and angle of the racks at that magical moment when the grown eel divines that now is the time to head for home.

The smoker sifted fine beech sawdust through his fingers and showed us tiny twigs of apple-wood. Their balance must be minutely adjusted to achieve the flavour he wants for smoked eel. Other products are oak-smoked. The production of this rare delicacy owes nothing to sophisticated technology. He adjusts the temperature by means of a hand-operated draught control and monitors progress to the point where the eels turn to a lovely copper colour by simply peering through a spy-hole. Success is the result of human judgment and skill patiently acquired. You could see what Auden called that "eye-on-the-object look" of the man with a real vocation.

Church Fête, Piddletrenthide

Nearby Yeovilton was recorded as the hottest place in England, so we went south down the little road that runs beside the River Piddle in search of cool shadows and running streams. The Piddle Valley is narrow. Often there is barely the width of a single house on either side, so that elongated villages – Alton Pancras, Piddletrenthide, Piddlehinton – are stretched out thinly towards Puddletown and Poole harbour. Cottages are built with alternating horizontal bands of flint and brick, and roofs are made of thatch.

At Alton Pancras, cows were crowding against the rail to drink from the stream that runs in a gully beside the village street. We stopped at Piddletrenthide, where the Church tower, thick with pinnacles and gargoyles, stands up from a grassy churchyard across the river.

The river ran fast and clear under the bridge. The Church Fête was due to open at 2pm in the grounds of the manor. Already, with a quarter of an hour to go, there was a queue of 50 or so, and 20 cars were parked in the meadow where an odd octagonal structure, now a crumbling, overgrown ruin, windowless but stylish and ornate, looks down from the edge of a wood. Someone told us that it had been a "mirror house", built as a diversion for the folk from the manor, and that a cut from the river had made an "eel inlet" into the manor grounds. There were trestle tables on three sides of the lawn, attended by ladies in wide-brimmed hats, and a marquee for flowers and vegetables. The heaviest marrow weighed 8lb 14oz. When everyone was assembled, the vicar, in panama, clerical collar and khaki shorts, bade us all welcome.

Industrial Frome

The first time I came to Somerset was by train from Paddington, in a "slip-coach" that was detached from the rest of the train at Westbury, Wiltshire. The first stop I noticed over the county boundary was evidently a sizeable town, identifiable when we came to a halt as "Frome, the home of Chedlet Cheese". As a child, I had loved those soft segments of processed Cheddar wrapped in silver paper, so ever since I saw that sign, I have had good feelings about Frome.

This week, artists from the surrounding villages have centred on the Round Tower in the town, which is now a gallery but was built as a "scouring furnace" for treating wool when that was the commodity that made Frome rich. At nearby Beckington, the handsome church on the hill, well-made terraces of weavers' cottages and stately clothiers' houses give a sense of this area's wealth at a time when the local weaving business was largely a cottage industry, often a family enterprise combined with work in the fields.

We climbed up one of Frome's steep streets to where, around 1665, a speculative builder started to encroach on the surrounding fields to build housing specifically for workers in the clothing trade. Work was beginning to be done by larger, organised groups of labourers concentrated in the town. In the district called Trinity, the orderly streets such as Wiltshire's Barton and Trinity Row, and the neat courtyards, are a survival of very early industrial housing and make it possible to understand how Cobbett was able to describe the then teeming town of Frome as a southern Manchester. But sturdy, Somerset country-folk were resistant to too much technological advance, and Frome remained itself.

Native and Continental at The Show

The Gillingham and Shaftesbury is a one-day show, and this year, its 68th, the day was blustery with squally rain. By mid-morning there was mud underfoot, and at each downpour people dashed, dodging the golf umbrellas, for the nearest covered stand.

In a sunny interval, I was watching finalists in a beef-cattle class. My neighbour at the fence, a seasoned observer with a practised eye, identified the breeds. There were cream-coloured, rough-coated Simmentals from Switzerland and enormous, smooth-coated Limousins from France. He regretted the dominance of these Continental breeds and others, such as the Charolais and Belgian Blue, in British beef production. But his eye brightened at the sight of a big, proud, dark-red animal. It was a North Devon Red, he said, representative of a fine old native breed. The Romans noticed "Red Rubies" grazing our western hillsides and, until the black-and-white invasion came and Friesians colonised our dairy pastures, they were successful milkers as well as beef cattle, and the source of Devonshire cream.

Next, I went towards the sound of a brass band, and was surprised to see men in Lederhosen and a saxophonist with a curly moustache of stupendous size. They were a 12-piece Bavarian band, enthusiastically received by the local crowd. But, as with the beef cattle, local breeds were not to be eclipsed by the Continental competition. The Gillingham Silver Band, soberly uniformed, was proudly maintaining one British musical tradition, while in a crowded entertainment tent, the Yetties, an unfailingly popular West Country folk group, were just as effectively maintaining another.

On the River Gascoigne

The little river Gascoigne rises near the hamlet of Milborne Wick, wriggles through the ancient "rotten borough" of Milborne Port, and completes its course of around five miles by spilling into the Yeo just before that river spreads out into a handsome ornamental lake below Sherborne Castle. At Milborne Port, a bend in the Gascoigne used to be the home of a notable company of ducks that stopped the traffic twice a day by waddling slowly up the length of South Street to be fed. This spring, the river has been the focus of nature-watch in at least two gardens. In one, on a curve of the river, a single water-rail, normally a highly secretive bird ("much more often heard than seen", the book says, and looking like a moorhen with particularly long legs) openly made its winter home, and fed with the familiar garden birds.

Downstream, in a secluded garden enclosed by fences, where a few years ago a family of hedgehogs was reared in a compost heap, a mating pair of mallards was seen flying in repeatedly this Spring. Then, in June, a visiting black Labrador called Bertie, trained to the gun, wandered into a shady corner under a willow, and created a sudden commotion in a flower-bed. The female of the pair flew up and revealed a clutch of 10 eggs in a nest buried amongst the hardy geraniums and "lady's mantle". She seems to be untroubled by friendly human interest, and leaves the nest briefly morning and evening to fly off – presumably to the water, which is some 30 yards away. The eggs are safe so far, and should hatch before long, but ducklings here are vulnerable to rats, and it is not clear how this brood will get past the barrier of fences to the river.

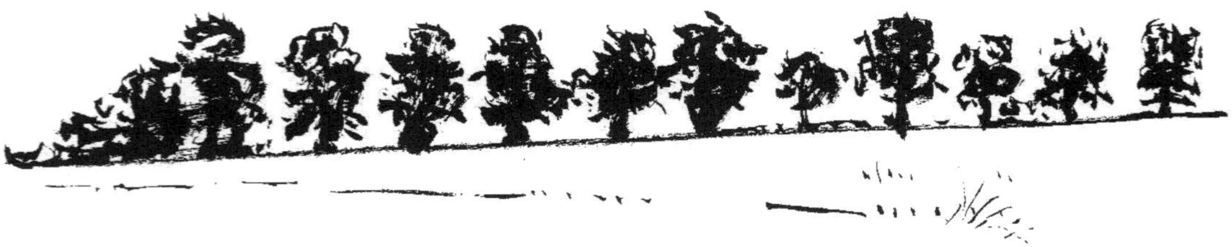

Boscastle and Thomas Hardy

We were 120 miles from home, near the sea in North Cornwall. It was a landscape of steep valleys with rivers and gullies winding down over slate and shale and through gaps in the buckled and twisted rocks to the sea. We had arrived at our destination, the porch of an old rectory, after a three-hour journey. In 1870, to travel a similar distance and arrive before nightfall from near Dorchester, Thomas Hardy had had to rise from his bed at 4am and travel by foot, train and pony-trap to this remote hamlet. There he was received at this same porch, in its "little dell", down a path that "dives under the trees like a rabbit's burrow" by the "young lady in brown" who was to become his wife.

By chance, we were in Boscastle almost exactly one year after the floods. On that warm, thundery afternoon, almost five inches of rain had fallen in a few hours on ground already saturated, and a strange roaring sound had been heard as the run-off from the high slopes funnelled down past the rectory, part of the deluge that devastated the harbour village. On this trip, we walked down to a scene of absolute peace at St. Juliot's churchyard, over the stone stile from the field, where a man was keen to share his concern that last night's heavy dew was impeding his rotary mower. And then to the harbour itself, the river now trickling safely in its deep channel, under the two bridges, past thriving shops and restaurants, towards a flat sea. Here, a fishing boat moved quietly into an entrance so narrow that boats rowed by nine men used to be needed to tow sailing craft safely in between the rocks.

Finds in the Film Archive

So far this summer outdoor events have been drenched by rain, but two indoor events have given us contrasting windows into country life. At Bruton, an eager crowd assembled for a showing of salvaged archive film. We watched a royal visit, early this century, to Warminster. The streets were packed with people. Everyone waved a flag, except the policemen, who parted the crowd to make way for the procession of cars, and the older men, who deferentially raised their hats. The commentator pointed out that everyone had a hat and that no one was overweight. Next, we watched a man on the Mendips extracting snails from dry stone walls, and supplying them to a restaurant. In another clip, two men with dogs were after livelier prey among the rocks at low tide near Watchet. Conger eels bucked and reared as the dogs tried to fasten on to them. Somerset and Dorset trains steamed through farmland, and men grew withies for basket-making or mashed barrels of apples into home-made cider.

The following evening we were invited to a village in Dorset, and went down through teeming rain to the tiny hall where seats were set out in a shallow semi-circle facing a low platform with two chairs, a guitar, several kinds of accordion, a drum and a small lyre. There were readings with music from Vita Sackville-West's poem, The Land. The audience was held enthralled for an hour and a half by this compelling recreation of country life a generation ago. The programme noted the poem's "unsentimental absorption with the unending conflict and collaboration between man and earth – a relationship whose imbalance has become of great concern to 21st-century mankind". There were smiles of recognition from listening farmers at the poem's sharp observation of scenes they themselves knew so well.

The Friar's Journey

When we visited Woodspring Priory near the coast beyond Weston, we read that in 1317 a friar of the Augustinian community there, one Thomas Taverner, had been found to have behaved badly in the choir and, having failed to respond to penance and flagellation, had been sent 40 miles across Somerset's varied terrain to exile in Bruton.

It would have been a remarkable journey. When he had got beyond the salt-marshes where the priory stands, he would probably have headed for Axbridge – then a town of substance, walled and fortified in Saxon days. His likely route would have taken him on towards Cheddar, where King John had maintained a residence. He would have marvelled at the immensity of the limestone cliffs climbing 400 ft above his winding path through the gorge. Although bishops and abbots had been draining the marshy lowlands since the 12th century, Taverner would probably have kept to higher ground. He would have seen the distinctive shape of Glastonbury Tor standing up from The Levels, though without the now familiar tower on its summit. Church and earlier tower had been shattered by a landslip in 1271.

Whether or not an erring friar might have expected succour from monks at Wells, he would have passed through the city and stood in the space now called Cathedral Green gazing in awe up at the gallery of saints, bishops and kings on the cathedral's great west front. His onward route lay through Shepton Mallet and Evercreech, around the shoulder of Creech Hill, and down into Bruton. Neither the packhorse bridge nor the abbey wall had yet been built. Taverner would no doubt have forded the river at the spot where I picked my way over the stepping stones last week going towards where the priory is thought to have stood.

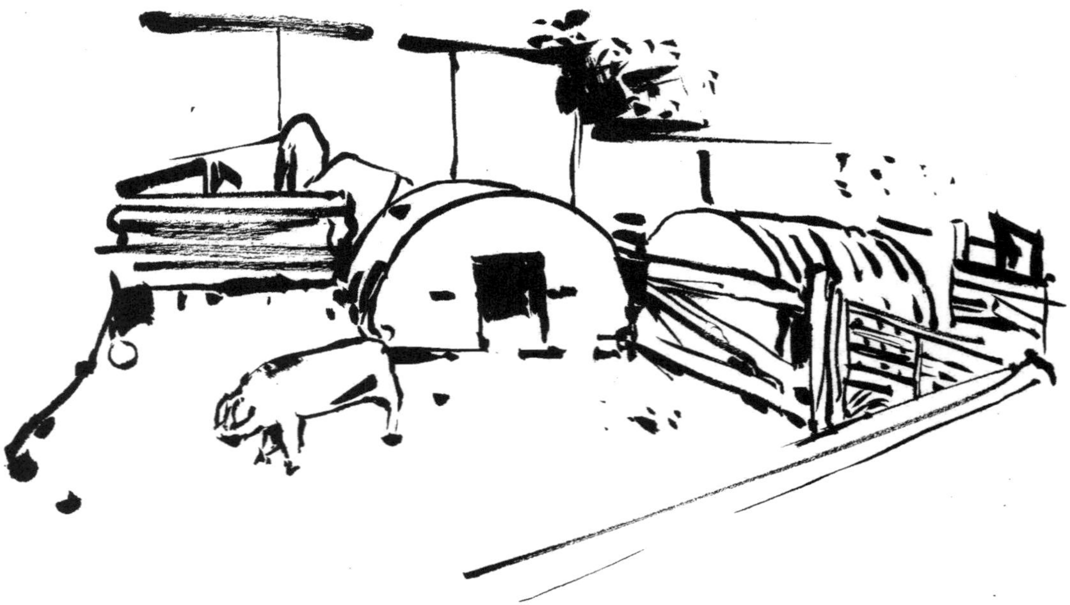

Ancient Sites

It was well before the heavy summer rains, but already, at the summer solstice, a grey morning looked unpromising for the enthusiasts assembling at Stonehenge, Glastonbury and Avebury, while we set off to visit other ancient Wessex sites. Our way to the Iron Age hillfort of Badbury Rings took us through dark and dripping tunnels of overhanging trees, across flood meadows beside the Stour near Blandford, then up into chalk hills and along the two-mile beech avenue, whose lines of trees are said to number 365 on each side and which leads towards the great house at Kingston Lacy. We walked the track up towards Badbury's three concentric rings of ditches and ramparts, stopping to look back across wide swaths of arable land to the west and into the mist to the south. Locals say that on a clear day they can see the Isle of Wight. The natural chalk grassland surrounding the ramparts derived its character from thousands of years of grazing. But grazing was suspended during the second world war, scrub returned, and the fine grasses and wildflowers were overwhelmed. Now the National Trust is grazing the land again, with sheep in winter and cattle in summer.

By the time we had reached our second site, Maiden Castle, outside Dorchester, the mist had turned into steady rain. I had often seen the castle's silhouette from a distance but had never before been close. Its Celtic name, Mai Dun, means "great hill" and now, from nearby, the scale of its giant outline against the greyness was hard to credit. It is one of the largest hillforts in Europe and covers 47 acres.

Dorchester had, a few minutes earlier, been obscured by the weather. Now towers re-emerged, and a more recent settlement – Prince Charles's model village, Poundbury – revealed its trim outlines.

Natural Drainage on The Levels

News stories had told of thousands of homes flooded in the north, and of 40 families made homeless in Gloucester. But we had heard no word of flooding from our local wetlands, the Somerset Levels. Their great expanse, encircled by hill ranges and the sea, is like a spongy saucer with a great capacity to absorb, but since human settlement began the inhabitants have lived with the threat of flood, especially when high tides in the Bristol Channel have coincided with exceptional rainfall. In 1607 the sea walls were breached, 100 square miles were flooded, 30 villages submerged and 65 people killed. Human ingenuity has constantly worked to reclaim land for agriculture. A typical square mile of The Levels is said to contain 21 miles of drainage channels.

Coming, as we do, from South Somerset, the first bit of authentic levels scenery we see is the causeway that joins Huish Episcopi to the raised settlement of Muchelney, with low, flat land on both sides, pollarded willows lining the roadside channel on the left and a cider orchard on the right. The roadway was dry there and we saw no flooding from the relative height of the grassy island where Muchelney Abbey's ruins stand. From the vantage point of Langport churchyard, high above the plain where the rivers Yeo and Parrett meet, and sometimes swell out to make a sheet of water miles wide, covering all but the treetops, we saw the rivers quietly contained between their banks, and cattle untroubled in fields bounded not by hedges but by ditches and streams. At the visitor centre they said that pumping had not been necessary. The dry spell in the spring had made land and rivers receptive and combined with the rural lack of concrete and tarmac to enable The Levels to cope with all that June's weather had brought.

Pen Selwood Horse Show

I was late arriving at the Pen Selwood horse show and the loudspeaker was already announcing an early prizewinner: "Emma Hamilton on Gin and Tonic" as the contestants in class 3 ("leading rein, eight years and under") were parading. One small rider peering out from under her big hat was led by her brother, who said she was three years old. My neighbour in the crowd pointed out her granddaughter, aged four, who had won her class at Stourhead last year. I asked how much a pony cost. "Don't ask," she said.

At the next ring it was novice show-jumping ("for riders who had not previously won a class – jumps not to exceed two feet three inches"). Although one horse was big enough to get over the obstacles with little more than a walking step, others, tiny ponies with small and utterly fearless riders, were racing in at terrific speed and making heroic leaps. "They frighten the life out of me," said a passerby. But there were no mishaps. A woman leaning on a gate watching the quieter pursuit of dressage told me she had ridden as a girl. She loved to go to local shows, watch others, and be among horses again. She approved the skill of the girl tackling the intricate dressage course. Bryan Young, the retired farmer who started the show 30 years ago, said that this was great horse-riding country. You can ride for miles through woods towards Stourhead without using a road. He was chairman of the Pen Selwood Sports and Social Club. The horse show, run by volunteers, was one of its five annual charity fundraising events. Sadly, there was no cricket or football now, but the 10-mile road run survived and followed a circuit through surrounding parts of what was once the great forest of Selwood without meeting a single intersecting road.

The Scythe

After a good, dry spell, giant tractors rumble through the lanes, hauling the apparatus of modern grass-cutting. Livestock farmers want to secure a good supply of silage. But in one particular field in Muchelney, I watched a weatherbeaten young man, barefoot and lean, with flowing hair and beard, plying a scythe – mowing as men did before such work was mechanised. He worked with a rhythmic, repetitive action, knees slightly bent, head steady, weight smoothly transferred as the scythe swung back and through, delivering a swift, clean and even cut, low to the ground. This was surely the very sight that, in the 17th century, prompted Andrew Marvell to write in one of his mower poems: "Thus he threw his elbow round / de-populating all the ground."

At a pause to take his whetstone from its holster and hone the blade, the mower said that his scythe, as well as being quieter than mechanical alternatives and needing no fossil fuel, was also quicker and less tiring to use. Also, after each swathe was cut, it left the mown grass in a straight, neat line (a "windrow") readily turned with a fork.

This was the West Country Scythe Festival. A competition between scythe and strimmer proved him right. In the set time, the strimmer cut, noisily and roughly, about two thirds of the area neatly and silently cut by the scythe. To achieve such a fine cut, the curved cutting edge must meet the blade of grass at just the right angle and be very sharp.

Another young enthusiast introduced me to the technique of "peening", painstakingly hammering the leading edge of the blade against a small, rounded anvil to achieve the right profile, after which a fine stone gives the razor-thin finish. He had learnt about scything in the Pyrenees, where it is an essential skill for subsistence farmers who cannot afford machinery and who work small fields on remote slopes. The nimblest and lightest scythes are Austrian, and Continental.

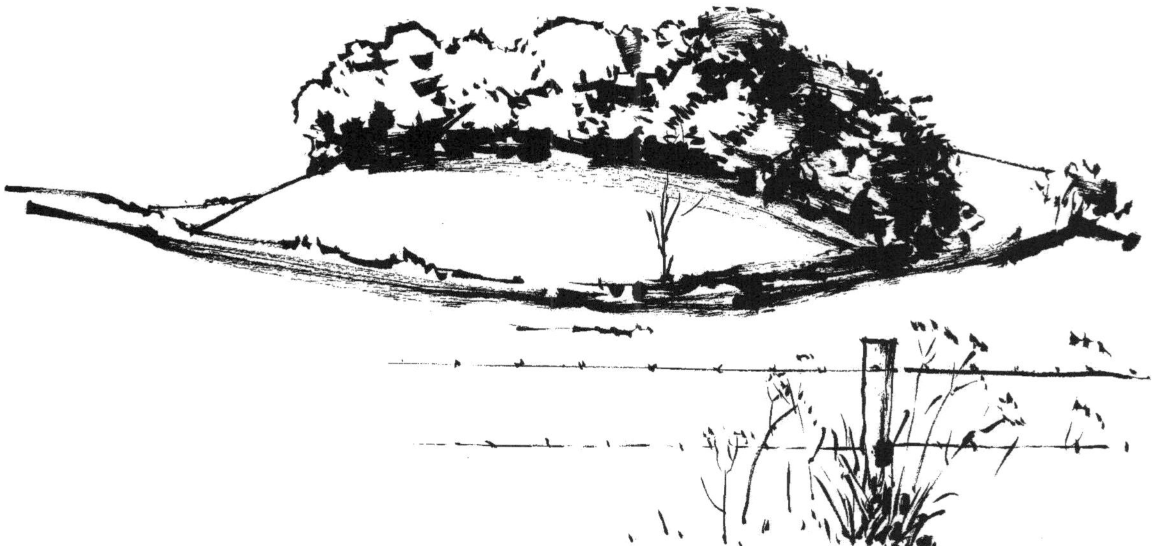

Birth of a Princess

For a good many years, a glance down into the valley below where we live has shown us three ponies in a paddock enjoying an apparently settled and sociable life together. Duchess is a 13-year-old Dale/Fell cross, Dusky a New Forest pony of 33, and Crumble a 27-year-old Shetland. But last year Duchess was introduced to Bashful Bobby Dazzler, a traditional cob stallion with a temperament so gentle that even a child may lead him out, a strikingly handsome appearance and a tally of many prizes at the shows.

The resulting pregnancy was Duchess's first, and she was healthy and characteristically placid throughout the 11 months. Towards the end, a camera was set up in her stall to monitor progress. At 5.30am on 18 March, she was sleeping peacefully, so the camera was switched off. At 7am she was again seen to be sleeping peacefully, but now there was a bright-eyed foal beside her. The foal, white with darker patches, took more of her appearance from the piebald stallion than from the roan mare. Duchess showed no anxiety about human contact with her young, named Dazzling Princess, but now the threesome was a foursome, its dynamic changed.

Dusky at first took such a close and friendly interest in the foal that Duchess was uneasy, so mother and foal were kept apart from the others for a day or two. Princess could wander with her mother, gallop, or kick up her heels while the others watched. But very soon the four were at ease together, Princess and Dusky often grooming each other, and all of them competing joyously in the evening stampede when called in by their owner. Princess's markings are getting darker, almost chocolate brown. She is nearly as tall as her mother and almost as handsome as her father. Maybe she too will have a future at the shows.

Dewpond

At the heart of Ashmore, Dorset's highest village, up on the chalk of the Wessex Ridgeway, is the celebrated circular dewpond. Framed by the houses, cottages and barns grouped round its grassy edge, it makes a satisfying picture. Dewponds like this one, said to be 1,000 years old, were natural or manmade depressions, lined with straw, clay or chalk and fed by rainwater. They used to provide water for livestock, and their maintenance was achieved by the trampling of the animals and the periodic digging out of the silt, which was spread on the fields as fertilizer.

I was drawn back to this particular pond by the Blackmore Vale magazine's statement that it "had reached crisis point last year when it became clogged with silt, algae and unwanted fish". Dairy farms, whose cattle daily drank at the pond, have gone. Sheep used to drink there too, but now have water piped to their fields. The goldfish population is another contributor to the crisis. The 12 introduced in 1993 multiplied to the point where 4,500 were re-homed in 2007, and more than 1,000 are estimated still to remain. Their voracious appetite destroys invertebrates, plants and plankton that would otherwise keep the pond clean. I saw two young boys fishing with nets, but it was hard to see the fish in the reddish murk of the water and they caught nothing.

The companies of housemartins that skimmed the surface for insects were more successful, even though a survey in 2007 showed that this impoverished pond had only five species of insect per water sample, whereas a healthy pond has 26. But the renovation group is now delighted. Continuing fundraising will enable them to start the work that will, they trust, revive the pond and preserve it for another thousand years.

Coppicing

In a barn at Piddletrenthide, the man I had come to see was enjoying his customary fag and coffee before moving off to the coppice that has long been his place of work, though now, he says, coppicing, for him, is more like occupational therapy than work. We bumped down a perilous track in his wagon to where four and a half acres of hazel were divided into compartments, each in a different year of growth up to the seventh, which is the time for cutting. He nurtures each generation of young shoots, and then harvests them by the traditional coppicing craft, cutting the wood back down to the tree stumps to make way for new growth. On the sunnier slopes, a seven-year-old hazel gets to a height of about 6 metres (20 ft). Most go to make spars for thatching now that there is no call for wooden sheep hurdles.

When I went in among the stumps, he told me to look out for adders. A while ago, his rough-haired Jack Russell had failed to respond to his whistle and been found inert under the wagon, bitten by an adder. Happily, she was got to the vet in time for the antidote to work. Deer are a plague in the coppice; they find the tender young hazels appetising. He showed me a kink and joint low down on a young sapling where a deer had spoilt the true, straight growth.

We looked at the clean, precise cuts he had made. When he started he was taught that you must cut with an upward slanting stroke of the sharp hook. If you gave a downward cut you might split the wood and let in rain, leading to rot, and if you used a saw rather than a hook the new growth would be poor. Later on he conducted his own experiment, cutting half the crop with a hook and half with a chainsaw. The ensuing growth was equal in both halves. But he still believes in the upward cut.

Country Music brought to Life

Two villages, Ibberton and Belchalwell, lie side by side under the shadow of the Dorset downs at the southern edge of Blackmore Vale. We had been invited to their village hall to hear about a little book from this very place that had come to light in an antique shop and was to be brought to life again. The title page reads: "Benjamin Rose, his book, January 29 1820." It is a beautiful manuscript collection of country dance tunes, some unrecorded elsewhere, many unlikely to have been heard for very many years.

We learned that the writer had had a smallholding in Belchalwell and run an ale-house. Some of the older folk in the audience recalled his descendants and knew which fields had been his. He was only 24 years old when he wrote the title page. How had he come to have the skill to write out musical notation so neatly that it sits elegantly on the page and can be read with ease?

In the interval, we drank tea outside as a warm, low evening sun spread long shadows across the hillside. Then the musicians unpacked their instruments: several fiddles and assorted squeeze-boxes, a cello, a harmonica, guitars and a serpent – the instrument celebrated by Thomas Hardy in Under the Greenwood Tree: "Old things pass away, 'tis true; but the serpent was a good old note: a deep, rich note was the serpent." We were to revel in the serpent's deep, rich note and the fact that neither Benjamin Rose's music nor the serpent's authentic note had altogether passed away. The musicians played with verve and joy. When copies were handed round and someone set a tempo, they combined with effortless skill and no fuss at all to bring to spontaneous life the very music that the folk of Belchalwell, forbearers of some of those present, had heard 200 years ago. And it might never have been heard again.

Rare Vintages

Forget the picture of fuddled labourers reeling in fields at harvest time after draughts of the farmer's rudimentary cider. The cider-maker I was visiting at East Chinnock is as much an artist as any maker of fine wine. I came upon him in a shady barn, looking like an alchemist in his cell, with flasks and pipette, calculating the sulphur content of a golden fluid that was to be distilled to make cider-brandy, the Somerset Calvados.

But the product I was going to taste was another that he had been refining for years. He began making cider in 1986 from local apples, and planted his own orchard 15 years ago. By 2004 he thought he had almost reached his goal – a bottle-fermented cider, "petillant", closer in style to Normandy's "cidre bouché" than to English types, a light, refreshing drink with tiny bubbles and a little edge. Then a barn, containing 1,000 bottles, caught fire and his stock was ruined. It was a catastrophe, unexplained and undeserved, worthy of a Hardy novel.

So he began again, and now we were sitting at a long table outside the farmhouse, in early evening sunshine, sampling the results of his loving toil. These were ciders that had won top prizes at county shows. Between the four we tried there were distinctions – one a shade drier, another fuller and more rounded, one with a delicate hint of elderflower.

As we sipped and chatted, I learned that in Napoleonic times when claret, like all things French, was anathema to the English, cider was drunk by discerning gentlefolk. In the 17th century it had been bottle-fermented and enjoyed by Charles II. People who call in at this farm thinking to buy a flagon of rustic scrumpy will be introduced to something of a different order.

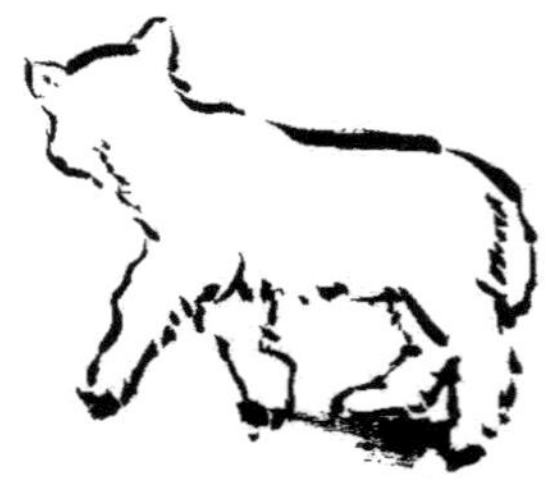

Fruit Farm

I had passed through villages called Ash, Highway and Coat, in territory unknown to me close to the river Parrett, when I caught sight of the name New Cross and pictures of cherries on a board, which told me that I had arrived at my destination, once a typical Somerset mixed farm where cattle roamed, but in this generation a fruit farm. There are two good reasons for growing fruit hereabouts, near South Petherton. The protection of surrounding hills and ridges like the Poldens produces a balmy micro-climate, and a specially helpful soil retains moisture.

The fact that one field, now given over to gooseberries, has long been known as the cherry orchard and that old villagers used to talk of the great cherry trees that once grew there tells of local fruit growing in earlier times. But I was taken to see ranks of modern cherry trees. Several varieties were all growing on Gisella 5 rootstock, which keeps the trees compact, and under frames of netting to keep out the birds – mainly blackbirds, though this year, mistle-thrushes, too. Only one kind of tree needs no such protection. The Morello cherry, grown for the making of liqueur by a neighbouring distiller of cider brandy, is so tart that birds will not touch it.

Twelve young people from Romania and Bulgaria, here on a six month scheme for seasonal agricultural work, were, with the farmer's wife, carefully picking each cherry from its clump, identifying and discarding any that were split, and retaining the perfect ones in their satchels. They were working intently on Sweetheart cherries before moving off in their wagons to the long tables outside the barn for a cheerful mid-morning break. It looked like a scene from Provence. A good, warm spell at flowering time meant that fruit was ready to pick ten days earlier than usual. Cars brought eager buyers for farm gate sales of hand-picked fruits as well as things like honey and apple juice, and the asparagus looked inviting too.

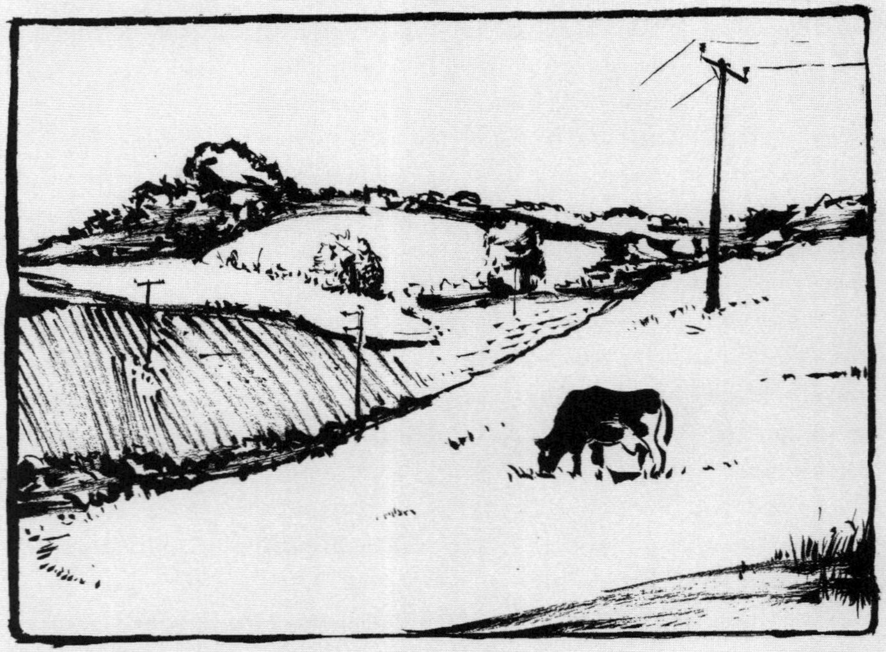

AUTUMN

The Prosperous People's Village

In March, there was the hedge-laying competition, when a favourite 250-yard length of hedge nearby lay docked, trimmed and pegged – a skeleton with no sign of active life. Now, in early autumn, you approach it through a dark tunnel where willowy new growth arches and meets overhead. When you get to the particular length of hedge, and recall the March scene, it is almost impossible to relate it to what you see now. The footway is barely passable; long, shaggy nettles lean over from either side. Feathery grass grows head-high in the banks. Lacy hedge-parsley, long, pendulous, blue-green docks, puffy dandelions and white bindweed flowers, fluted like lilies, grow profusely on either side. From the sycamore hedge itself, sappy new shoots have thrust vertically out of their straightjacket. Already they reach head high and more. There will be plenty for the hedge-layer to do next time. Further on, beside the metalled road, the grassy banks are neatly mown, and an elaborate wrough-iron gate shows the formal garden of a big house. From the top of the hill, in the open sunlight, you can see into Wiltshire and Dorset to the east, across the marshes. Five horses walk past, three with women aboard and two straggling behind, like Thelwell ponies, carrying helmeted little girls. There is a wooden sign board on the left, at the open entrance to a group of stone barns and stables, all 18th century or earlier, and well-maintained. In white letters is the word 'Wilkinthroop'. The book of Somerset place names translates this as 'the prosperous people's village'. There is a giant Van Gogh sunflower near a field of maize. The sheep now look just a little woolly, not as naked as a few weeks ago. It is necessary to back onto the bank to make way for two slow tractors pulling wide trailers stacked with bales of hay. In the sky a large hawk is wheeling slowly up in the thermals, then scudding a long, straight stretch on the breeze. The prosperous folk chose a good place for their upland settlement.

Blackmoor Vale and Tess

After weeks of heat with scarcely a breeze, a rough wind brought an autumn scene in a moment. Red and brown leaves, tinder-dry, covered the bank, hiding the sparse patches of spiky brown grass that were all the drought had left. Hardy says that the fields of "this fertile and sheltered tract of country" are never brown. When he bicycled along the lanes, he can never have seen a summer like this one. In 1924, a gardener at Marnhull saw an old man with a bicycle looking over the gate at a thatched cottage and asked if he could help. "No thank you" said the visitor, "I was only seeing where I put my Tess". The text of Tess of the D'Urbevilles makes plain Hardy's love of Blackmoor Vale ("an engirdled and secluded region, for the most part untrodden as yet by tourist ...") though he admits that "an unguided ramble into its recesses in bad weather is apt to engender dissatisfaction with its narrow, tortuous and miry ways." He would be pleasantly surprised to see how little time has changed Tess's village. No tourists are evident. Tess's cottage is hidden up a quiet path where a shaggy, black-faced sheep, which stumbled down the bank in front of us, and some sleepy cattle over the hedge, were the only living creatures we saw. The length of the walk from "the Pure Drop" Inn explains why Tess's father preferred to drink at Rolliver's, now a substantial private house. He would be sad to see the old brewery building semi-derelict. But there has been little change to the buildings of Church Farm, by the cross-roads, and it is easy to follow the probable path of the "young men of a superior class" who were spending their Whitsun holidays on a walking tour through the Vale of Blackmoor, and who joined the few local "idlers and pedestrians" gathered round the spot where the village girls, dressed in white gowns and each carrying a peeled willow and a bunch of white flowers, joined in their May Day ritual. It could almost happen today.

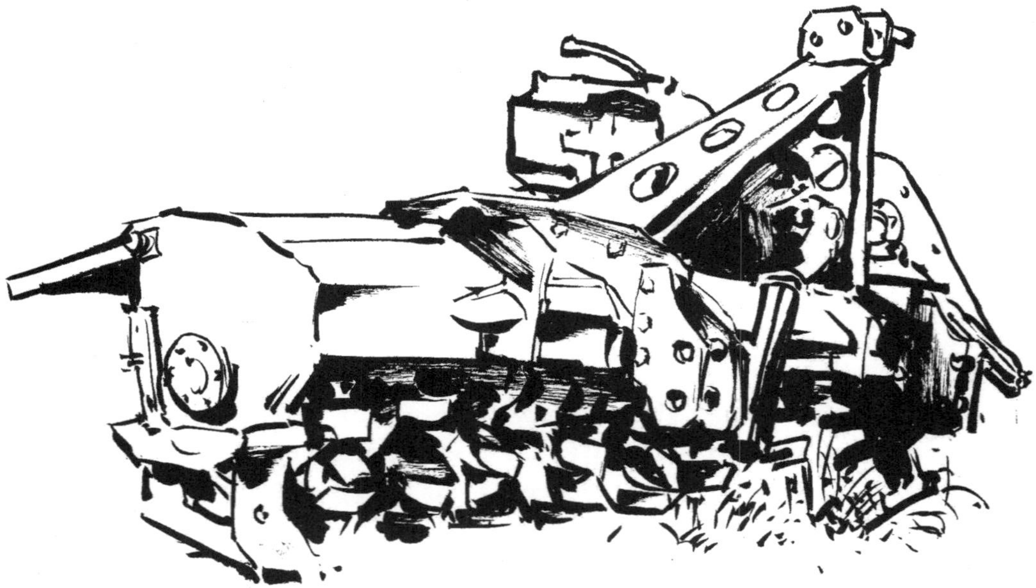

Mills

Big tractors with lamps like searchlights work long after dark to bring in the harvest, and a monstrous engine makes short work of wide fields of maize, cutting and chewing the crop, leaves, stalks, corn-cobs and all, and sending an accurate shower of small particles into the hopper of a tender that runs alongside. In the garden, the grape harvest looks promising, though April frosts did some damage, and local fauna – perhaps squirrels – did more. Production levels will certainly exceed the first year's five bottles, and there is hope that the weeks of Mediterranean sunshine will be reflected in the quality of the vintage. Most of the grain from this area goes to Wessex Grain, with huge silos like nuclear installations at Henstridge. The firm handles more than 50,000 tonnes in a year. Local mills no longer have a function. Visitors from Lincolnshire, who lived within sight of Boston Stump, talked of all the mills near their home. To them, a mill was a windmill. When we lived in a weaver's cottage on the moors above Haslingden, with a view of the sea beyond Preston, the word "mill" meant the satanic kind. Our neighbour had, as a girl trudged down the lane in her clogs to one full of clattering looms. But here, a mill is a watermill. You do not expect windmills in Somerset, though there is a truncated one, now a dwelling, beside a road across the Polden hills, and at High Ham, not far away, we found another. It has a thatched cap, which is a rarity, and, with a fair wind, used to grind 300lb of meal in an hour. It was built on a circular earth platform, to keep wandering sheep or unsteady farmers from harm when the sails were turning. Names of local farmers, and notes of the amount of meal their bags of grain yielded, are still recorded on some of the timbers.

The Pack Fair

Each day, gusts of wind blow larger holes in screens of foliage. We see bits of sky that have been hidden since the spring and cannot rake fast enough to keep up with the fall of red and yellow leaves. And there are other familiar marks of autumn. The carnival placard is up again at the roundabout outside Wincanton. Throughout the summer, reversing the natural cycle, people have been hibernating in barns and school halls, refurbishing carnival floats with fantastic designs, devising new themes, sewing on sequins and rehearsing tableaux, so that now, each town in turn can transform itself on one Saturday night for a glorious mardi gras. Sherborne, six miles away in Dorset, has its Pack Monday fair. I thought the name derived from the pack horses with which travelling pedlars and quacks arrived like Autolycus to scatter nostrums and knick-knacks amongst the peasantry, so I went early on a damp Monday to see what happens nowadays. There were traders' stalls, generators throbbing, men stretching tarpaulins and plastic sheets against the drizzle, and a few early customers peering at knitwear, burgers, cutlery, watches and mobile phones. One medieval touch was the stall selling bright velvet jesters' and harlequins' hats. Cheap Street winds down towards the Abbey where I found a copy of Sherborne Scene with an article about the origin on the fair. A popular local myth claims that the abbot who rebuilt the nave instituted this fair to celebrate the day when the work was completed and workers packed to leave. This has, it seems, no foundation in fact. But it was at Michaelmas fairs that agricultural workers assembled, wearing the smocks of their trades, and hoped to be hired for the season. If a man was chosen, he made a "pact" or contract with the employer. The great gathering naturally attracted traders and entertainers and in time developed into the Pact fair.

Friends of the Station

You have to look carefully at the pitted tarmac to make out the fragments of concrete and stone that mark where the station building used to be. It was a handsome, even gracious, stone structure. Now there are just two mean little bus shelters. The footbridge necessarily survives; eight up-trains still stop here every day, though a surprising number of townspeople do not know that they can easily take a rail trip to Weymouth, or go in the other direction, via Westbury, to Bath, Bristol or London. The Friends of Bruton Station, 20 volunteers, have revived memories of the times before the 1968 demolition, when Ina Parsons, the booking clerk, faced a bright, open fire across the waiting room and exchanged a rich stock of local information with customers. And when Ern Baker, the porter (in buttoned serge waistcoat) was said to owe the permanent tilt of his head to all those years spent listening for the down-train to round Sheephouse bend. But the "friends", though conservationists, are not motivated by nostalgia. They aim to help revitalise the station as a practical asset, and the railway company, South Wales and West Trains, is spending both cash and man-hours on a joint effort with them, supplying materials for repair and refurbishment, and arranging for two of their employees, whose efforts are normally spread across a great many other scattered, rural stations, to join the local work parties on their scheduled day. The enterprise reflects an initiative taken by district and county councils to revive railway use as a contributor to the local economy. The "friends" have cut down over-grown vegetation, trimmed hedges, established troughs of shrubs, and planted foxglove, nigella and hollyhocks. But they have also circulated up-to-date timetables in the town, and already more people are finding their way up the hill to the station.

The Bowflock

There is evidence of seasonal stirring, not only in the great molehills that are seen, each morning, to have erupted in the lawn, but also in the mountains of combustible material being piled high for Guy Fawkes night – traditionally the optimum time for the most productive coupling between ram and ewe. The ram wears a shield or pad on his chest. It has on it a dye which shows on the rump of each ewe he has covered. The shepherd notes the dyed rumps and the date, 147 days later, when the particular ewe is likely to lamb. I re-visited the 'Bowflock', a specially attractive and lovingly-tended flock of Shetland sheep. Exact forecasts of likely lambing dates are less crucial with Shetlands than with some breeds. They come from a long history in bleak, Northerly places. Their spare, athletic build, small size and remarkably fine fleece equip them for independent survival and they are good at lambing unaided. If you run you hand down a sheep's back (an action which makes tails wag with evident pleasure) you can feel how the finest wool is at the shoulder and there is a progressive coarsening towards the rump, because, in their natural habitat, they huddle together for protection against icy winds with their backs to the blast. The Bowflock, enlarged this year to 33 animals, mostly ewes, now lives in relative luxury. They have moved away from the small, exposed hillside where I first saw them. On some mornings last winter, their owner, who has to fit their care around a full-time job, could not get up the steep track through the ice. Now they have 10 spacious acres of an ancient ridge and furrow field, lush with nutritious, green grass, on lowland beside the Fosse Way in the peaceful village of Babcary. This year, a champion ram from Wiltshire will have moved in before Guy Fawkes night.

Wyke Champflower

A mile or so out of Bruton, on the way to Wells, the road emerges from amongst sizeable steep-sided hills to a spot where a single, much smaller hill, notable for its conical shape and treecapped top, stands up on your left. Below it lies the hamlet of Wyke Champflower – six farms, the manor, Wyke House, and a few cottages, spread across a relatively low, flat space. The River Brue wriggles westwards, under a fine old stone bridge with pointed arches.

Wyke's population of around 100 is thought to be as high as it has ever been. The little church is built onto one end of the long, low manor house. Revisiting it, I recalled watching families from farms and cottages walking to church, and small children (now with children of their own) clambering with books and toys into the tall boxpews where, once the door was shut, they could read or play unseen until it was time to walk home again.

The squire used to read the lesson and take the collection. A plaque set into a wall facing the churchyard now commemorates him: "Duncan Mackenzie of the Mackenzies of Red Castle in the Black Isle... scholar of Winchester and Brasenose... Resident in Jaipur, Jodhpur, and Hyderabad." Across the churchyard, inquisitive young Friesian heifers peer over the fence at the gravestones or up at what Pevsner describes as the "fanciful" bell-tower. The church is only 46 feet long from end to end, but there, inside, stands the lofty, carved stone pulpit, fit to grace a great town church. Up in the tiny panelled chancel, two people dealing with mouse droppings on the altar recall Sir Duncan's days with affection. They say that people still make cheese and go to church in Wyke.

Apple Day

The weekend Guardian tells us that the hectarage of apple-orchard in the country has decreased by two-thirds in the past 30 years, so it was good to make a rough count of 205 different species of apple laid out on trestle tables at the Dorchester Apple Day. Each one's card gave its name and provenance: "Mornington Pearmain – arose from cider pomace in the garden of Mr Turley, Uckfield, 1770..."

"Striped Beefing – we found in the garden of W Crowe at Lakenham, Norwich, 1794." Around the hall were set out every kind of apple product – ciders, chutneys, jellies, Dorset apple cake, and of course, principally, and in all their variety of colour, size, shape, texture and flavour, the English apples themselves. And there were free tastings. "Apple Days" are joyous celebrations. And it was not just apples.

"Life in the slow lane" was the legend above a stall advertising escargots. There was "New Forest Nectar" and beside it, with more ginger and bite to it, the companion beverage: "Ginger with attitude". "Dorset Blue Vinny" was but one of the local cheeses whose smiling, proud and expert makers were eager to offer samples. At the International Tree Foundation stand, I was struck by the story of Richard St. Barbe Baker, who, in 1922, founded a group in Kenya called "the Men of the Trees".

Fifty warriors were sworn to plant and protect trees. The society that grew from that beginning has achieved planting programmes in Palestine, a conservation programme in American Redwood forests, a reclamation scheme in the Sahara, and much more. And all because a wounded ex-soldier with a degree in Divinity cared about trees.

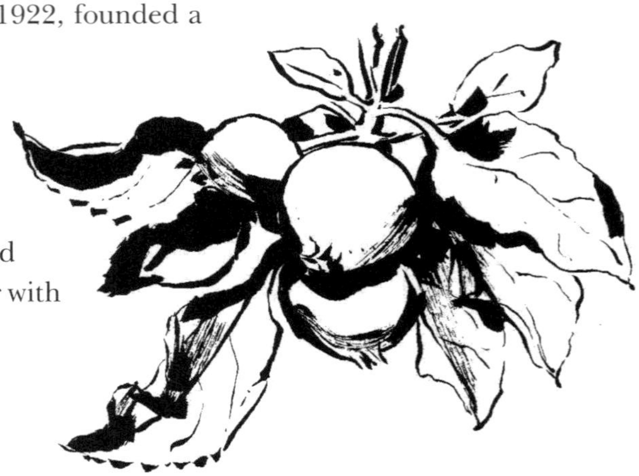

Farm Sale

By the time I got to the farm-sale, it was hard to get a footing at the waterlogged entrance to the field marked "Car Park". Inside, items of farm machinery were scattered across a big space.

There were tractors, trailers, muck-spreaders, ploughs, harrows, a yard-scraper and a concrete mixer. The auctioneer had by now moved into the barn to dispose of the stock. This was a County farm of 140 acres with about 90 milking cows, and was for sale because the long-term tenants were to take semi-retirement.

The sale had attracted a big proportion of the farming community from miles around. It was a popular social event, an opportunity for friends to gather, reminisce, and show their regard for a family that had worked hard and done well. There was satisfaction that the County was not to sell the farmhouse for profit or the land for development. This will still be a working farm. A good crowd was gathered for the cattle auction; the first to be sold, the best milkers, were fetching 500 or 600 guineas.

The cows had not been milked that morning so as to be shown with udders full; some of them were already waiting to be let in to the milking parlour. They enjoy the milking; it is a relief, the parlour is warm, dry and familiar, and a ration of palatable cake is released when the cowman pulls on a rope. One of these cows had learned to twist her neck round, pull the rope herself, and so get an extra delivery of cake. This herd, described in the catalogue as having "good feet and tidy udders", was to be dispersed in bits and pieces later in the day. Now they must adapt to new environments, groupings and pecking orders. It may take time to learn how to get extra cake.

Sturminster Newton

A meadow down by the Stour was filled with rows of parked cars, and the stalls on the recreation ground were buzzing with activity on the Saturday morning of the Sturminster Newton Cheese Festival. You might have thought you were at the hub of a thriving national cheese-making industry. Yet, a short walk away, down by the overgrown site of the cattle market, the derelict remains of the town's once famous cheese factory made a sad contrast.

Formerly a local farmers' cooperative, it had latterly been owned, and then two years ago closed down, by Dairy Crest. The cattle market had been closed five years earlier. Since cattle market and cheese factory had been central to the town's commercial health, you could have forgiven the townsfolk if local pride and confidence had failed. But, back on the recreation ground, crowds were pressing forward to see the demonstration of farmhouse cheese-making. There were 20 local producers of meat, eggs, pies, fish, honey, ice-cream, cider and fruit. And it was the very fact of the market's closure that first stimulated people to look for imaginative ways of re-using the site and revitalising the town.

A scheme for an ecological centre gave rise to a group called "Sustainable Sturminster". Their display demonstrated solar water-heating and other environmentally friendly techniques. A task-force called Sturquest aims to bring together those interests that can best combine to revive the town. "Stur's" serious aims were advertised by the Town Crier, himself a former Dairy Crest employee, now resplendent in a new uniform made by his wife.

A Pigeon called Jeremy

Most of the summer's agricultural shows were cancelled because of the foot and mouth outbreak, but the September Frome Show went ahead, albeit without livestock, and gave the local farming community a late opportunity for a congenial gathering and sharing of woes.

"Nothing like a show to bring on the rain," said a voice in the car-park, and the Mayoress needed a golf umbrella to keep herself and her chain of office dry. Magnificent Shire horses were the only big animals on show, so, instead of admiring giant Charolais bulls or prolific Gloucester Old Spot sows, people gazed longingly at gleaming tractors and expensive cars available for those whose credit rating had survived in good shape.

The first creature to catch my eye was a disabled pigeon called Jeremy. He was being tenderly nursed by two young girls in the Larkrise Community Farm tent. This farm was set up some 12 years ago as an extension of a special needs school, and is now an independent charity. The farm manager is the only employee, and depends on voluntary help to run courses and look after 46 large animals – horses, cattle, sheep, goats and pigs – and a fluctuating population of rabbits, guinea-pigs and birds, including, now, Jeremy.

The family that found him in their garden, bedraggled and unable to fly, contacted Larkrise, who took him in and identified him as a Welsh racing pigeon. His broken wing could not be mended, so the owner did not want him back. He now walks at leisure around the farm and is accepted on friendly terms by the turkeys though not the geese. And he has recently acquired a companion; another pigeon flies in daily to join him on his walk.

Village Store Revived

Our supermarket's new extension will provide a noodle bar, rotisserie, pizzeria, worldwide takeaway, fishmonger, butcher and patisserie to add to the plenty already available. But in the smart, newly fitted stockroom of Maiden Bradley's resurrected village shop, I was shown just three kinds of shampoo on the shelf (as against 30 at the supermarket) and proudly told that each one was stocked in response to a particular request from a resident, like the leaf tea imported from Harrogate specifically for one valued customer who preferred to drink no other kind.

In the summer, the previous owners gave two months' notice that, as income from the shop and post office was insufficient, they would close in September. After this date, the nearest post office was at Horningsham, only 3 miles away but with no bus link. An open meeting revealed a passion to keep the village shop open. There was a quick and positive response from the District Council and Countryside Agency. The next step was to form a Friendly Society, and by late October the Maiden Bradley Village Shop Association Ltd was duly registered, so that share certificates could be issued to the 100 shareholders.

A share costs £5, and each shareholder has one vote, irrespective of the size of the holding. Grants and the capital raised from shares have funded the relaunch, a questionnaire has informed purchase of stock, and voluntary labour has made the shop bright and welcoming. Staffing for the hours people want is part paid and part voluntary and Consignia will reopen the post office counter soon. Other villages are looking to follow Maiden Bradley's example.

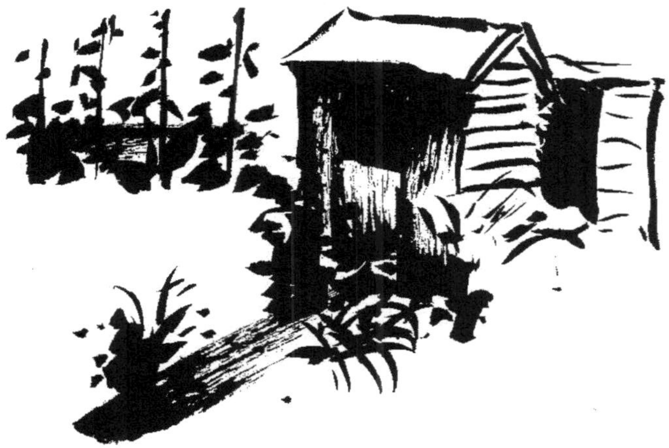

Bound Apprentice

Last week, the one person I know who was born and bred in the village showed me an elaborately inscribed document dated January 28 1908, the form of indenture whereby his father, the son of a sawyer, was bound to "put himself apprentice" to a blacksmith, "to learn his art, trade or business" and "faithfully to serve his secrets". His pay was to rise, over four years, from 2/6d to 5/6d per week.

Recollections of that apprentice's later life, after the war in which he served and his brother was killed, make windows into a local life in which people went on foot, where horsepower and steampower were still important, and the rhythm of the farming year informed the pattern of daily life. The story goes that on one fortunate day he asked a girl who was walking by to hold the head of a horse he was shoeing, and thus began an acquaintance with the gamekeeper's daughter which duly ripened into romance and marriage. Later, he worked on the railway as a platelayer. He was a big, strong man, well equipped for the heavy work involved, and became a "ganger" or foreman. At haymaking times, when the men got home in the evening, they would set to with wooden rakes and pitchforks as the rick was expertly built and thatched by hand. Such work was unpaid, but the children fetched and carried jugs of drink, and they had rides on the wagons or even on the slatted elevator that sloped up to the top of the rick. Now, a generation later, convoys of giant, gleaming tractors from regional contractors rumble along the lanes with machinery that makes short work of whole prairies of grass at the touch of a lever.

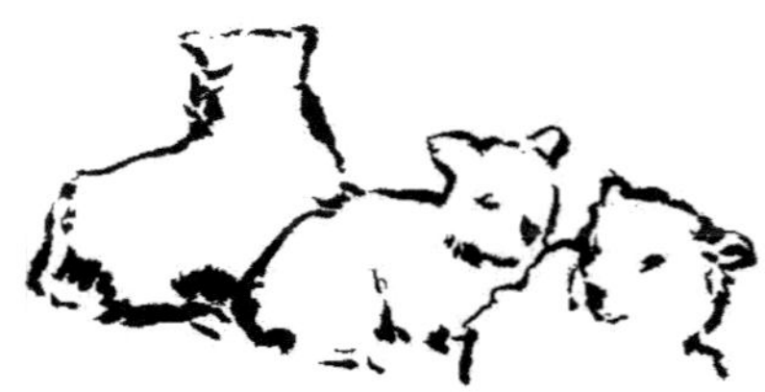

Heavy Horses

After August, when the nights get longer and the dews are heavy, cut grass for haymaking takes time to dry. I saw a seven-acre meadow where the grass was mown on a Wednesday in mid-September, and turned successively on the Thursday, Friday and Saturday (all good, sunny days), so that by the Sunday morning it was dry enough to be baled. Then an old grey Ferguson tractor was coaxed from its retreat under a hedge to get the hay – nutritious winter feed for the horses – into the barns.

I saw a similar tractor in the lineup of agricultural machinery at the 27th Wessex Heavy Horse Show and Country Fair. There were stationary internal combustion engines, too, of one and a half horsepower, puttering away to demonstrate how they would pump water or drive a saw, or – as one owner and operator explained – be turned by an ingenious deployment of belts and wheels to any task on the farm that required a little power. And there was the raw manpower of the axemen. Built like hammer-throwers, they swung heavy axes with minute accuracy to make deep cuts in vertical logs set up like giant tree trunks.

But this was really a show for the heavy horse enthusiasts, celebrating farming's traditional power source – magnificent, glistening Shires, Clydesdales, Percherons and Suffolk Punches, showing their paces in the ring. A display panel depicted the heavy horses on one smallholding, still pulling disc harrows, seed drills and ploughs. A man and two Shires walk 11 miles to plough an acre with a single furrow. And at least one brewery still delivers ale through its home town by horse-drawn dray. Its horses sleep on a bed of moss peat, eat six buckets of feed a day when working, and have a self-catering holiday in August.

Isle of Purbeck

Our route lay over the light grey sand of a track that meandered across heathland on the Isle of Purbeck, through gorse, spiky grasses and purple heather, with patches of pine and birch – territory like that of the New Forest, on similar soil not far away beyond the waters of Poole Harbour.

It was a grey day with rain threatening and each gust of wind dislodged a few more brown or yellow leaves, though not enough yet to make a carpet underfoot. We were looking for the "Little Sea", marked on a map of 1721 as just a small saltwater inlet between dunes on the edge of Studland Bay. But this is a stretch of coastline where, in places, land is gradually extending itself into sea, as sand is washed ashore by wind and tide, trapped by grasses and colonised by plants. And in this way the Little Sea has been cut off from the sea over the centuries to become in modern times a land-locked, freshwater lake.

What we thought was the right track dwindled and then petered out, so we struggled straight ahead through a thicket of fir and holly, until suddenly there was the stretch of chilly water, ruffled by the wind and lapping at our feet. Back at Studland, St. Nicholas's Church, part Saxon, mainly Norman, stands up against the sky on raised ground, and has a feeling of massive permanence. A leaflet directs attention to the wildlife in the churchyard and the variety of colours and patterns in the lichens growing on its walls and ancient gravestones, explaining that the abundance of these organisms, specially sensitive to pollution, is evidence of the purity of the air.

We went down the lane to the beach, a long white curve, and saw Old Harry Rocks away to our right. There, the sea eats away the chalk, carving out tunnels and separating great pillars from the cliff face.

The Ploughing Match

The 60th annual Western Area Ploughing Match was being held the day before Plough Sunday in sight of the tall tower of St. Buryan Church on a treeless plateau a few miles in from Land's End. Fields divided by ancient "hedges" made of granite boulders, were marked out in numbered rectangles, and eager crowds were assembling early. Competitors had come from as far as Birmingham and Monmouthshire, and it was a great day out for folk from nearby. We went first to the magnificent pairs of Shire horses, some elaborately decorated with brasses and plumes, and asked a spectator what we should look out for. He had travelled from Oxfordshire where he worked six Suffolk Punches, and drove a wagon, conducting revellers up and down hill on "pint to pint" expeditions. He embarked on an explanation of the points system for scoring ploughing contests and soon lost us in the technicalities, but infected us with the same bright-eyed enthusiasm that everyone there seemed to share.

We watched the blade making a clean incision, turning the first sod, and cutting a straight furrow at just the right depth, pitch and angle – tools and skills honed over centuries to frustrate the weeds and yield the best crop. If the horses were the more picturesque – tossing their heads and wheeling round in a tight circle at each end with impeccable teamwork – the tractors were impressive, too. A driver positioned his tractor, one wheel in a furrow, then turned in his seat to make precise adjustments with a battery of levers before finally allowing the blade to slice into the turf at exactly the right spot.

When we went back to the horses, four generations of one local family – grandfather, father, son and grandson, all ploughmen and all contestants – were grouped for photographs with their Shire horses, Dawn and Darling.

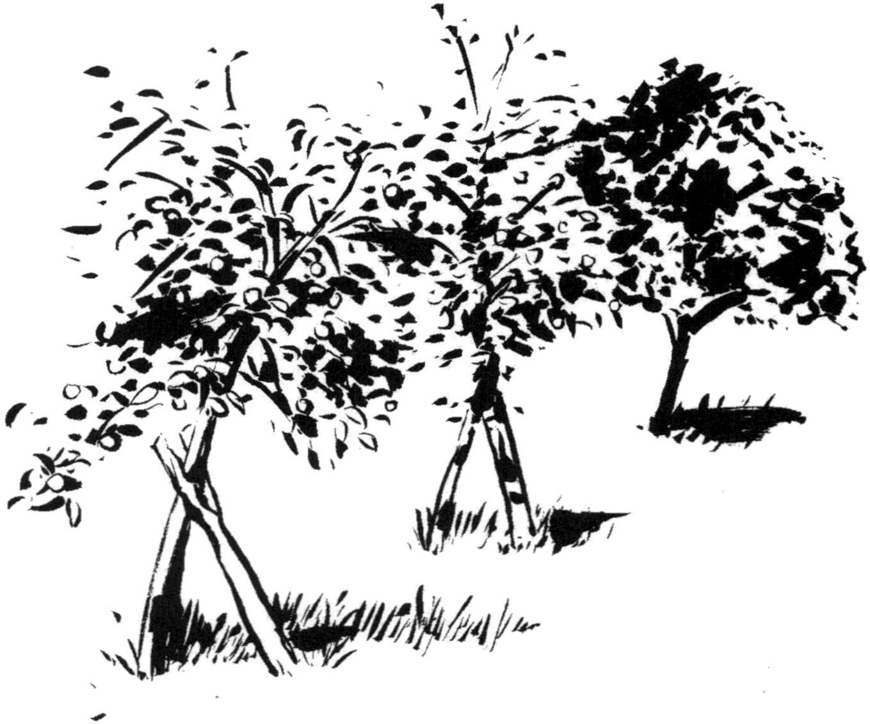

Community Orchards

I was looking for a particular and precious half-acre, tucked away in a small hamlet, where, on Apple Day (October 21), an ancient dew pond, revived after a long drought, was formally reopened to frogs, toads and newts by the president of the Dorset Wildlife Trust. I eventually found it some distance up a winding lane across the way from the bridge at Sturminster Newton.

This patch of ground is precious because it is Dorset's smallest wildlife reserve and the village's community orchard. In 1970 there were 62,000 hectares of commercial orchards in England. By 1997 the figure slipped to 22,000. As towns spread, and more fruit was imported, local species, as well as local fruit-growing skills and traditions, declined. But this orchard is safe; it was given to the Dorset Wildlife Trust with conditions that protect it from development.

As a community orchard, it is open to anyone from the village who wants a quiet place to sit, an apple to pick, or a job to do, such as pruning or hedge-laying. Some of its trees are ancient. One, called "Belle de Boskoop", has partly fallen but still sends out new growth and produces fruit. Another, said to be the oldest, combines "Autumn Pearmain" with a bittersweet cider variety, both grafted on to one root stock. There is a dead plum tree useful to nesting birds and a rotting log pile favoured by insects and other small creatures.

Deer, badger, fox and rabbit visit, and the Little Owl hunts here. Among the abundant wildflower population, the "Corky-fruited Dropwort" is listed as a notable Dorset species. And among the apple information provided in the shelter is the fact that the cogs in the machinery of the famous mill at the foot of the hill are made from apple wood.

Morris Dance

On a Monday evening we visited the Gaggle of Geese, a pub tucked away in the Dorset village of Buckland Newton. The big yard and grassy space made an ideal setting for the Wessex Morris men's performance. This was almost the last evening of their season, which began at dawn on May Day when, by custom, they dance on the giant's hill above Cerne Abbas, parading the Dorset Ooser – a horned head on a pole.

Morris troupes, or "sides" have three officers – the squire, the bagman and the foreman. We were to meet the foreman, who teaches the steps and movements. A scholar in the traditions of "the Morris", he sat us down to a beer, as dancers and spectators began to assemble and assured us that there was no hurry as "Morris mean time" applied. He regards theories that relate Morris dance to ancient fertility rites, and interpret the waving of handkerchiefs and clashing of sticks as attempts to frighten evil spirits, as no more than interesting speculation.

He was full of information about Morris's recorded history, its decline during the 19th century and revival in the 20th. He pointed out the white shirts and black breeches, the baldric with crossed bands across the chest, the motley tatty jacket, the sticks and the bells. But now he had to break off. Pairs were forming the first set, and he was to assume the role of the fool, weaving in and out of the dance, making irreverent comments, and waving a balloon on a stick, the modern equivalent of a pig's bladder and cow's tail. Long ago the music was made by pipe and tabor, but we had three musicians, on concertina, piano-accordion and melodion. Most of the tunes derived from the Cotswold tradition. Before moving on to the Hunter's Moon at Middlemarsh, they performed an old favourite – Bonny Green Garters.

Cornish Mines

We are back from a week in the far west – high above Sennen Cove and a short walk across windswept clifftops from Land's End, with a wide view of Atlantic weather racing in towards the striking silhouette of Cape Cornwall. The proud tower on the summit is a chimney built for the prosaic purpose of improving the draught to the boiler-house of the mine below. Since the Bronze Age men, women and children have toiled to get tin here, and also copper and arsenic; first from the alluvial gravels and later from mining the deep, narrow, mineral-rich veins or "lodes" embedded in the granite. We went along narrow streets between terraced cottages in the old, grey mining town of St. Just, looking for a way down the precipitous Cot Valley to the narrow inlet at Porth Nanven. There, almost cut off from the land behind you, and fronting foaming waves that crash into the rocks, you can understand why early travellers from mainland Europe believed they had reached the edge of the world.

Back at clifftop level, you can walk the tracks through tussocky grass, bracken and gorse towards the tall, gaunt ruins of engine houses that made deep-shaft mining possible and powered the pumps that drained water from below ground when mining was mechanised. There are the remains of alleys, chambers and plinths, now partly overgrown, where the rock was pulverised and sluiced, and ore roasted in a "calciner" to extract arsenic. The work involved great hardship and peril – two engine-houses sit on ledges only a few feet from the waves. One of them powered the winding gear of the Boscawen diagonal shaft that ran half a mile out under the sea. They say the miners could hear the movement of boulders on the seabed above their heads. Eight men and a boy died when the winding-chain broke in 1863.

High on the Mendips

The highest point of Mendip, at 316m above sea level, Beacon Batch commands the surrounding lowlands through all the points of the compass.

High Mendip country is generally regarded as bleak and desolate, but when we were there autumn sun made even hard, grey limestone look warm and welcoming. The terrain around Charterhouse is ankle-twisting country, with lumps of exposed rock, potholes and hidden depressions, signs of the scraping and burrowing for lead that has shaped the place since before the Romans came.

Their roads stretch like ribbons across wide spaces of bracken and tussocky grass. Around 1850, the industry was revived with an influx of Cornish expertise, and in a copse, we found heaps of rubble and fallen masonry, now overgrown with bramble, relics of a dwelling called Bleak House, where the Victorian captain of mines once lived.

Further downhill, we came to a dam beside a beach of shiny, black shale. But we found little sign of the dwellings of the miners whose muscles, picks and spades did the work, and who formed the Charterhouse community. The church still stands – evidence that a community did indeed exist here – and so does the school, which opened in 1881.

The schoolmistress's first entry in the log is for June 20: "Opened school ... no scholars presented themselves," but four came the next day, and in 1882 the average attendance was 13, though Mendip's harsher moods occasioned fluctuations; the log for January 1887 records that the children were dismissed because "I cannot get to my coal ... snow is up to my waist." One father said his three would come if they could, but "these cutting winds are enough to shram the poor little things."

Dorothy Wordsworth's Recollection

We were staying overnight with friends in the north west of the county, and their warning that we might be woken by the guttural bellowing of stags on the Quantock slopes behind the house made it clear that theirs is a different Somerset from ours down in the south east. The colour of the soil, too, and of the building stone, was a darker red than we are used to. Beside the church in the village, our eyes were drawn down a straight and formal drive towards the Classical façade – red brick with stone pilasters and pediment – of a great house. We were not brave enough to do more than peer in from the gateway. But Dorothy Wordsworth had been bolder. She records in her journal that on 15 April, 1789, when the house was still relatively recent, she had, as she often did, crossed the hills to 'Crookham' (more correctly 'Crowcombe'), and, on this occasion, 'walked about the Squire's grounds', noting 'Nature... trying to make beautiful what Art had deformed – ruins, hermitages etc. etc.' But despite her strictures on tasteless innovation, she did regard the dell as 'Romantic and beautiful'. Our own route, the next day, lay diagonally across the county, over the wide moorland of The Levels, along the spine of the Polden Hills, and back to the familiar green hollows and little rounded hills of the vale of Camelot. We took one of South Somerset's 'Health Walks' round the village of Queen Camel, past the row of thatched cottages (local, grey stone) in Grace Martin's Lane, and out into the soggy fields. Horses stood steaming beside the brook, and when we missed our way, a young girl, making her daily walk home from attending to her pony, pointed the way back to our footpath.

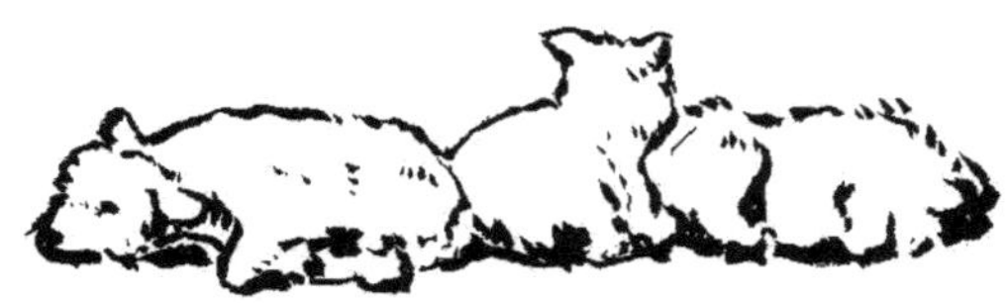

A Walk Round Bruton

The rainwater spouting from Bruton's gargoyles and gullies reminded me of a day in the 1960s when we salvaged what we could from Mill Cottage, down by the river, where murky floodwater was flowing in above the windowsills and the sofa was afloat.

But in the hills to the east, where the river Brue rises, the flood barrage, recently raised by two metres, has for many years successfully protected the town in the valley from floods. So, although the flow under Church bridge was fast, its level was low. I set out up the incline of Patwell Street to retrace what, 50 years ago, was a favoured route with the push-chair. Some way up I looked back from beside the mark of the flood level on 28 June 1917. I could hardly visualise the great sheet of water that must then have covered the lower part of the town.

The lane called Higher Backway took me to the top of St. Catherine's Hill. To the right was the spot where we once spent a cramped hour at dusk, crouching among prickly shrubs, suffering in silence and afflicted by insects, while waiting in vain for a badger sighting. But I went downhill instead, with a view of green slopes and ridges ahead, towards the Duck Walk. Close to where the stream divides were the tumbledown remains of a stone pigsty, now overgrown with brambles, where we used to lean over and admire an enormous sow wallowing in the mud. The old mill-leat, now the duck-pond, was brimming over, home to a busy crowd of waterfowl. My way went along Mill Dam and Mill Lane to Mill Cottage, now safe and dry. The names recall the five mills once driven by waterpower in the town. The Brue still drives Gant's Mill, which feeds electricity to the grid.

At the Show

At the Gillingham and Shaftesbury Show we paused at a tent surrounded by gleaming, blue agricultural machines to see a friend who knows the area's farmers, as he has spent his whole working life travelling North Dorset to sell tractors. He spoke of the trouble the long rainless spell (since broken) had caused, with only one good cut of hay rather than two or three. By Christmas, he said, fodder would be like gold dust. But there were positive signs too: a giant tractor bristling with sophisticated add-ons had a "sold" notice on it, and the farming folk sitting down to a ploughman's lunch and a glass or two had a hearty and contented look. Later on, Dorset was to provide supreme champions in both dairy and beef cattle classes.

An eager crowd pressed round the Turnpike Ring to watch a falconer training a young peregrine. A peregrine, he said, could reach a speed of over 200mph. This one, only eight months old, was very reluctant to leave his glove and perch on an assistant's while he slowly backed away to a distance of about a cricket-pitch length. Then, at a command, the bird was released, flew to the falconer's glove, and was rewarded with a piece of steak and appreciative applause. Next, the trainer stood farther away and twirled the "lure", a pheasant wing on the end of a line. The young bird swooped to a midair catch, earning a bigger reward and louder applause.

This is a great show for dogs and dog owners. There were gun dogs, fox hounds, hearing dogs for deaf people, and all manner of working dogs. We met a pair of big, amiable and beautifully groomed dogs with black, woolly coats. The owners told us they were Tibetan mastiffs, once bred as fearsome guards of herds and nomad camps. And the three tall, rangy dogs with sparse, wispy coats, lounging in the sunshine, were Scottish deerhounds, noted less for lively action than for spending long hours stretched out in comfort.

Farmers Market

After you have passed Penzance and the view of St. Michael's Mount out in the bay, the road to Sennen, the last village before Land's End, dips through some wooded hollows, but then winds across wide stretches of open moorland – bracken, gorse and granite outcrops. Here and there a track leads away to a grey-stone farm. From a distance, you can see the fine, tall tower of Sennen church ahead, and the imposing shape of the lonely Bible Christian chapel, which stands apart, far outside the village. But it was the school, with its welcoming sign and effective speed bumps, that we were bound for, keen to sample the Tuesday morning market (judged "Best farmers market of the year 2010" in the Cornwall Life food and drink awards).

We arrived early, but rows of cars were already parked on the football field, and there was a buzz inside the crowded sports hall. At the entrance, there was information about Ryeland sheep, a breed originally developed in rye-growing areas to graze and thicken the crop and increase the yield. The owner of a local flock showed us succulent cuts, and said Ryelands were laid-back and easy to manage. Behind every stall was a smiling enthusiast, keen to offer tastes of cheese, cooked meats, or cakes and bread fresh from the oven. There were mouthwatering piles of fruit, vegetables just lifted from Cornish soil, and Cornish cream, rich produce of those grey, coastal farms.

At one stall we bought crab pâté and learned about local samphire – rock samphire, not the marsh samphire we had once gathered on a Norfolk shore. Revelling in this celebration of the local harvest of plenty, we came to a stall selling cheese and found that two prize specimens of cheddar were remarkably familiar; they came not from Cornwall but from farms at Pilton and Ditcheat, close to home in South Somerset.

Life at the Mill Remembered

The town of Bruton lies below the southerly slopes of Creech Hill, so if you have lived in Bruton you take its great mass and singular shape for granted. With the familiar pattern of its wooded crest, there it is, a majestic backdrop to everyday life. But we were bound for the village of Lamyatt, on the other side, less familiar to Brutonians. We climbed the gradual incline past orchards full of sheep, by old stone cottages and farmhouses, and near the top found the church just below the woods which make that familiar shape along the crest.

After grey days of fierce wind and rain tearing the leaves from the trees, this was a quiet morning, with big areas of blue sky. From the top of the hill you could see across the wide, flat space below, past the slender tower of Evercreech church and out towards Shepton Mallet, Glastonbury and Wells. We went down the hillside to where the path to Milton Clevedon church goes through the farmyard, and a little farther on to where we had once looked for the site of a mill, now lost, beside the river Alham.

A reader, Rosemary Walker, from Hinton Blewett near Bristol, kindly sent the childhood reminiscences of a relative from the 1840s: "I never knew my dear mother till I was nearly six years old, for I was sent to my Aunt Allen who lived at Milton at the mill. My first impression is being in an orchard and seeing the big water wheel ... I remember a pretty mill stream and a field which came down to the mill. At the end of it was a farm house ... where farmer Giblett lived and we used to stroke down the oxen as they came in from ploughing. They had long horns tipped with brass, but they were so quiet we could fondle them."

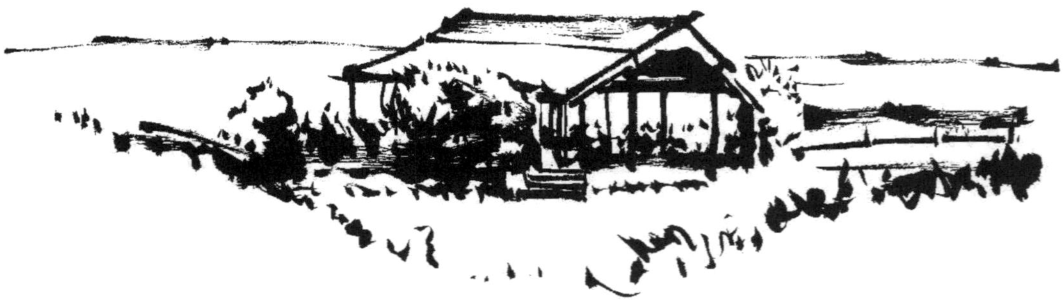

Brownsea

From the high seats in the coach going down to Poole for the crossing to Brownsea island we could see over the hedge-tops and across countryside ripening towards autumn. Some fields were already of russet coloured stubble, others striped with rows of cut grass lying out to dry, and ranks of hay-bales stretched across some of the slopes. Near Blandford we passed between broad, green water-meadows beside the river Stour, and after an hour we reached surviving patches of pine and gorse, relics of what was once wild heathland stretching across all the country from Poole to Christchurch, now almost totally built over by the continuous development of Bournemouth and its suburbs. Dorset heathland declined from 40,000 hectares in 1750 to 5,600 in 1983. Only on the Studland side of Poole harbour is the landscape still relatively wild and unspoilt, though Brownsea, one and a half miles long and three quarters of a mile wide, was utterly wild for a spell in the last century. In the 1920s, a reclusive owner despatched all other residents to the mainland, and parts of the island, long inhabited, began to revert to natural heath and woodland. Then, after the shock of a wild fire that burned for a week, she banned all public access to the island and retreated into a hermit's existence, allowing nature complete licence. After she died in 1961, aged 98, the island passed to the National Trust, which set about sensitive clearance and management of the woodland, open space, wetland, lagoon and beach. So now, after landing at the jetty beside the castle – developed from the Henry VIII's original defensive blockhouse – we were able to take the board-walk through the reed-beds, climb the pine hills on a carpet of cones looking for the indigenous red squirrels, and gaze across Purbeck and the harbour from the cliff-top, all the while with the sense of being apart, and on an island, albeit one that lies only a stone's throw from the unabashed affluence of the Sandbanks waterfront properties.

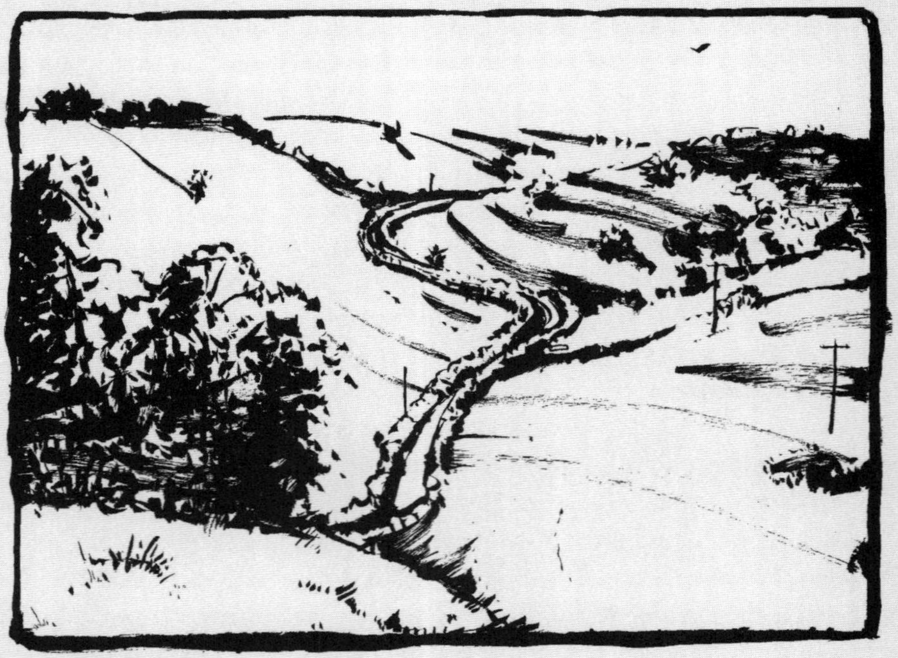

WINTER

Yarlington Mill

I was looking at a tall, gnarled apple tree in an orchard that had survived from the great days of Somerset cider-making. I asked how old it was. "At least 100 years". And what variety of apple did it bear? The answer indicated something of the importance of grafting in the cider-making business. This old tree bore Dabinett, Morgan Sweet, and Yarlington Mill. The last name caught my interest. I remembered a rustic nine-hole golf course at Yarlington. The shed that did duty as a club house was unstaffed. You collected your own drinks from a cupboard and signed for them in an exercise book. But the Yarlington Mill is a remarkable apple from what used to be called a "wilding", a tree that seeded itself in a hedge or odd corner of the farmyard. About 100 years ago a sapling sprang out of the wall by the mill-wheel at Yarlington. It produced an apple which became a favourite with cider-makers. In 1830 there were 35,000 acres of cider orchards in Somerset. Now, there are about 2,500. Apple juice concentrate supplies the gap in some commercial products. In 1970, there were five traditional cider-makers within a mile or two of Wincanton. Now there is only one, two miles up the road from where we live. Rosie's Cider operates from a collection of old cider barns and lofts, behind a "Somerset long-house" – medieval cottage in the middle (one up, one down, and a hole in the roof) with animal housing at one end and 18th century residential quarters added at the other. Now, the long, low thatched roof and the passage of time bind the three elements into one pleasing whole. It is a welcome neighbour in these days when almost every food or drink attracts a government health warning. We have authority in the folk wisdom of an old rhyme for the good this local product can do to ageing joints. "Wold Zam could never goe vur long Wi'out his jar or firkin; A used the Zider zame's were ile To keep his jints wrum quirkin".

Cider Making

There was a festival spirit on the Sunday when the apples were to be pressed at "Rosie's Cider". Relatives and friends dragged plastic sacks of apples towards the old wooden mill as the man in charge positioned an elderly tractor exactly so that the belt-drive turned the granite rollers at the right pace. The apples were all shapes and sizes; some were as big as Bramleys, others small and hard. We were told to throw out the really rotten ones. As the mill rumbled, crushing the first apples, someone had to operate a flat wooden spade, as if riddling the coke in a boiler, to shift lumps and keep the passage open. Then the pulp, or "pomace", was heaved with a big wooden shovel into the base of the press which had been lined with a sheet of nylon mesh. Another pair of hands levelled the pomace inside a square frame until it reached a height of around four inches. Then the nylon sheet was neatly folded over to form the first layer of the "cheese". Seven more layers followed through the morning, till the cheese reached up to the beam of the press, just below the roof of the barn. The mill kept on faithfully rattling and churning whilst some 50 sacks of apples (something like a ton weight) went into the hopper. A giant wooden cask was ready in the yard. I had to go before the moment when the press was turned, but I'm told there was a gush of juice down the channel from the magnificent machine (which dates from 1850: Maggs and Hindley, Engineers, Bourton). The 120 gallon cask was filled. A day later, there was still a steady trickle of juice and smaller casks were being filled. The screw was now wound right down, by capstan action with a metal bar, till the cheese had diminished to a height of a foot or two. Successful fermentation over the next few weeks will produce the traditionally health-giving local nectar which should be ready to drink about April.

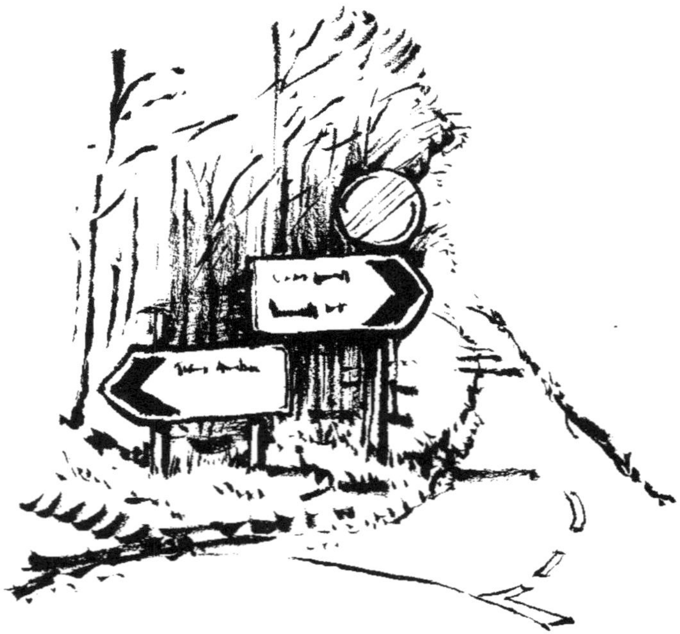

Blacksmith

A wheel mounting had come clean away from corroded metal on my rotary mower and, although the engine was in fine condition, I was regretfully loading the machine for its last journey to the refuse dump when I remembered the blacksmith. He made it like new in one day for £5. Down the road in Stalbridge is another blacksmith. The sign outside says "Established 1587". Geoffrey Jeans, now in charge, is a member of the founding family and his nephew is training to continue an unbroken tradition. At 9.30 in the morning the fire was flaring up from a small pile of coal-chips. I saw an accurate 16mm hole punched in the glowing red section of a flat metal strip. It was one component in the restoration of a complicated fence. Nowadays, the fire is fanned mechanically, though smoke still rises up the same, ancient chimney, one of two that form a blackened stone arch in the building that stands where it has always stood. Geoffrey's first job, after breakfast, when he was eight years old, was to ply the bellows. I saw him fashion a beautiful scroll, hammering the metal round the pointed end of the anvil. The business does not advertise ("People know where we are") but there is no shortage of work – not many horses to shoe, but still practical repair jobs for farmers or people like me. There is more in the way of chandeliers, curtain rails, decorative shepherds' crooks and garden arches. The place is full of relics of the time when metal implements were commonly hand-made to the particular requirements of personal customers. Outside is a great "bonding wheel" some five feet in diameter with an 18-inch opening in the centre. It was used in the process of fixing steel bands (or "bonds") to cartwheels at a time when a string of horses was usually tethered outside the forge.

The Brave Tin Soldier

A weekend when power lines were blown down, 40-foot waves hit West Country coasts, and, even in our sheltered corner, sycamores bent like bows, did not tempt people out of doors. But those who went were sometimes rewarded. At Muchelney, which lies at sea level, I walked a narrow causeway that showed precariously just above stretches of shallow, but ruffled, floodwater with reeds and willows straining against the gusts. This was not dangerous flooding, though groups of people nearby were wading ankle-deep with a wary and experienced eye on the River Parrett, where it swelled almost to the top of an embankment. They live against the inconstant rhythm of waters that encroach and recede rapidly in ways that are not predictable or wholly manageable. The land rises steeply up 70 metres to a ridge at Burton Pynsent, and a monument put up by the elder Pitt to commemorate the Pynsent, who bequeathed the estate to him in gratitude for opposition to a tax on cider. From these heights, there was a view across low moorland, cleared of cattle each winter before the waters come, a precious haven for waterfowl. The heronry looked desolate, but in February will be busy with nesting. Nearer home, in Wincanton, families with the spirit to battle through the squalls had a rich reward in the memorial hall. Fifty children, some no more than two years old, gathered on the floor and sat enchanted for an hour by the quietest live drama this Christmas. It visits village schools and halls, and its technology amounts to puppets, a tiny ring of bells, a tin whistle and a drum. The children were wide-eyed and open-mouthed at the story of the tin soldier with only one leg. They swayed in gleeful recognition each time the refrain came round: "He kept his chin up and looked straight forward because he was a brave tin soldier". Their journey was worthwhile too.

Prize Pigs

A new experience for me was the sight of a litter of 11 piglets, a few hours old, vigorously suckling a great sow. Right from the start the most dominant piglets suck on the front teats and a hierarchy is established with surviving runts at the tail end. The sow was a Large Black, the kind of animal a cottage family used to keep in the yard. These piglets were fathered by a white boar and are called Blues. They will be a pale bluish-grey colour with darker markings. The Blue has a nice balance of the various desirable properties like large hams or long loins for bacon. If you are assessing a pig, you look carefully at the roundness of the hams in relation to the relative fullness of the shoulder, the length of loin and (as I was shown), the way the animal walks. An obliging young "gilt" – a female that has not yet farrowed – walked away from us in a demonstration of how the feet must not be either pigeon-toed or too splay-footed. Pig farmers, like others, face problems. After the initial beef crisis, pork prices rose for a week or so, but consequent optimistic over-production then caused a drop. And there is a chance that regulations about the "mutilation" of animals may affect two traditional practices. Rings in the noses prevent pigs from rooting out grass and are important to safety when a large pig has to be manoeuvred. Notches in the ears are vital to proper identification when metal tags do not hold as well in pigs' ears as in cows'. Technology might solve the identification problem, but it is good to know that, whatever technology or the CAP may come up with, this producer works closely with a local butcher. If the butcher foresees that his customers will require a lot of fat bacon, the farmer aims to breed the pigs to yield it.

Compton Pauncefoot's Bells

The event that took me inside St. Mary's Church at Compton Pauncefoot, set in a hidden valley, with its perpendicular tower surmounted by a slender spire, was the moving of three ancient bells. The Treble and Second are probably 15th century, and the Tenor is dated 1627.

The Treble weighs over 5cwt and the Tenor, 36 inches in diameter, more than 8cwt. All three were found to be "very much in the state in which they were cast", in bronze, as I was told, (exactly 22% tin to 78% copper) and so perfectly formed by artists and craftsmen 400 or 500 years ago in moulds of sand, loam, horsehair and manure, as to sound through the centuries the true, ringing tones that please the ear. But the fittings were decayed by time and woodworm, and needed renewal if the bells were now to be safely swung rather than fixed and struck with hammers.

Each bell was lowered on to a wooden platform at the base of the tower by means of a block and tackle fixed to a specially fashioned steel beam that slotted into the masonry. Now, the task was to manoeuvre them over the medieval font without harm to either font or bell. One man, up in the tower, operated the block and tackle, lifting and lowering the great weight by fractions in response to shouted instructions from the master bellhanger below, while the bellhanger's wife worked the lever of a winch tethered to one of the nave pillars, following her husband's minute directions to edge the bell laterally, inch by inch, as he embraced it to make a human cushion.

Next the bells must go to the firm's workshops in Melbourne, Derbyshire; and the bellhanger and team travel to Melbourne, Australia, to work there on the peal of St. Patrick's Cathedral.

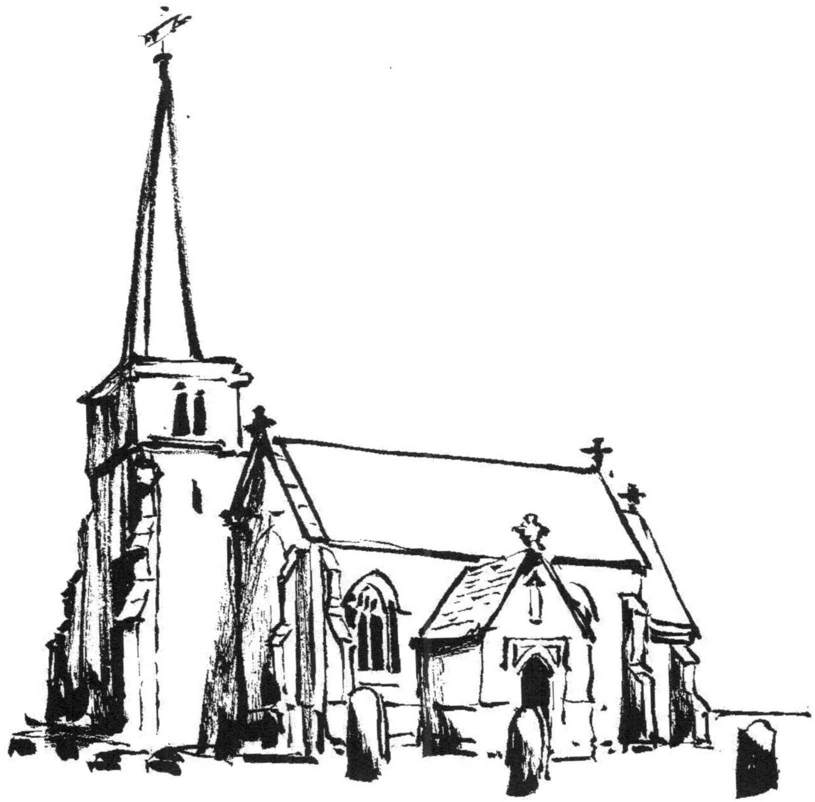

Hurdle Making

In a cottage not far from Tolpuddle, I met a young couple who, less than two years earlier (with two small daughters and a third child on the way), had been made redundant and given notice to quit their tied cottage. Now, the family – that third child was a boy – are thriving and happy, though they miss working with animals.

It is all to do with hazel wood. There used to be 25 hurdle makers in their tiny and remote village. Then agriculture changed, fencing could be cheaply mass-produced, and the ancient craft dwindled fast. To get rods of the right thickness, flexibility and strength to make hurdles, you need from seven to 10 years growth of wood; 35 acres, properly husbanded, would keep an old-time hurdle-maker for life. Since the craft declined, most of the woods are overgrown, but Jack and Anne Beckett saw potential. Overgrown tree-trunks make logs, which are cut, netted and sold on garage forecourts. The real work of Dorset Coppice Crafts, their firm, is in the skills of the hurdle maker, adapted to our times.

The wood must be stripped and split with a bill-hook, then woven by hand to create, not hurdles for shepherds, but panels made to size for gardens, dog-baskets, boot-racks, plant-climbers, rose-arches, and even chairs ("using carefully selected wood to achieve its natural curves... fully jointed – not a nail in sight").

A craft stand at the NEC led to orders from Japan and the US. Already it is hard to find enough suitable hazel to keep up with the order book. The firm has seven piece-work employees, including two lads learning the skills on the Welfare to Work scheme. And the traditional rotation of coppicing is restoring woodland, to the benefit of its flora and fauna.

The Odcombian Leg-stretcher

South Somerset villages tend either to tremble astride narrow roads that have become overloaded highways or, by contrast, to be hidden away, like those South and East of Yeovil that 'cluster in the combes and on the hillsides where the levels of central Somerset give way to a jumble of little hills, and age-old lanes have cut deep ravines in the soft, grey-gold stone'. Some of the sunken lanes have become tunnels, overarched and overgrown, making secret ways into and out of the villages. 'Chapel Hill', just wide enough for one vehicle, and twisting steeply down between cottages beside Odcombe Church, is one of these. An old tradition claims that the square tower of the church, on the crest of a hill, was once painted white and consequently, so far from being secret, made visible from both Bristol and English Channels. On a damp day I found it looming out of the mist, just visible at about 100 yards distance. Three horses with shaggy ankles and wearing winter coats stood close together just beyond the stone wall that encircles the green churchyard. In 1781 Odcombe had 92 houses. Now there are 337, and a modern estate near the church is called 'Coryate Close' after Thomas Coryate, the self-styled 'Odcombian Leg-stretcher', son of the vicar, who made stupendous efforts to lift Odcombe from obscurity by travelling, almost entirely on foot, to Venice and back in 1608. When he came home he hung the shoes he had worn all the way in the nave of the church, and wrote 'Coryate's Crudities, hastily gobbled up in five monthe travells… and newly digested in the hungry air of Odcombe'. The book did well, but the shoes disappeared and Odcombe seems content to have resumed its natural reticence.

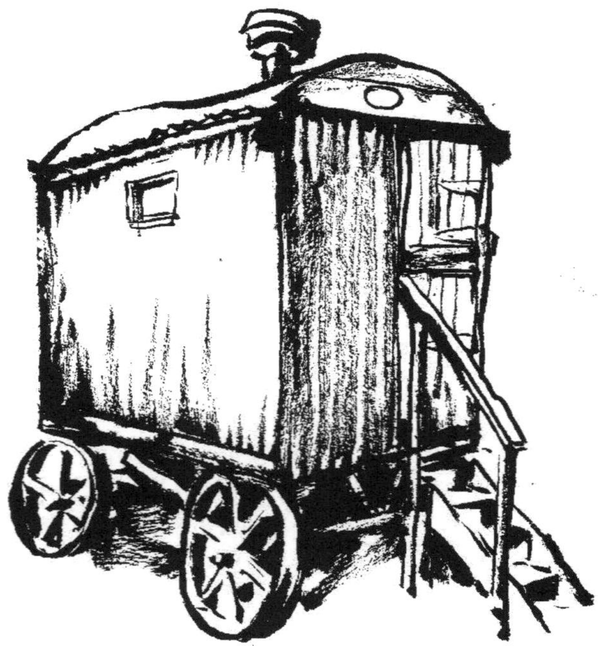

The Shepherd's Hut

At lambing time, the shepherd must be close at hand, and sufficiently alert, day and night, to know just when a ewe is going into labour. The expert can recognise uneasy rustlings in the straw and a particular kind of heave and grunt from the ewes.

Our local breeder of Dartmoors is employing traditional practice, but with some modern enhancements. The traditional part is that he uses a mobile shepherd's hut, very like that in which Thomas Hardy allowed Gabriel Oak, in the novel Far From The Madding Crowd, to fall into a stupor because the stove was smoking and the ventilating slide was unopened – carelessness which cost him his sheep. Hardy described Oak's accommodation as "a shepherd's hut ... presenting an outline to which an uninitiated person might have been puzzled to attach either meaning or use". The hut is 12 ft long and 6 ft wide, mounted on iron wheels 2 ft 8 in diameter. The chassis is formed of five strong lengthwise wooden members with heavy oak axle-beams. The body is of pine planks, gently arched, with a round opening for the chimney. Wooden steps are hooked on at the back, and there is a triangular metal draw-bar at the front for attachment to a traction engine.

The plate above the entrance names P&J Reeves of Bratton Iron Works, Westbury, Wiltshire, as the makers. Although it does not give a date, a local man of well over 70 said, 12 years ago, that he remembered this hut as having been in use "all his life". The modern enhancements include a modern wood-burning stove set on a metal sheet, a solid and new floor made of planks from redundant railway goods vehicles (the timber turned out to be mahogany), and a built-in wooden bed to replace Oak's "few corn-sacks thrown carelessly down".

There is also an electric baby-alarm set to convey to the slumbering shepherd the slightest sound from the straw.

Freedom in Mudford

If rainwater runs off the hills near Yeovil into the river Yeo's narrow channel at a time when the tide is in, the land at West Mudford can flood to a depth of several feet in a couple of hours. So it was good to know that those who, in 1710, built the farmhouse I was visiting, had set it on a little rise just so high that, even this year, the water never quite crept over the doorstep.

I had gone there to visit 12 hens in a paddock out behind the pigsties. They were evidently enjoying the extensive grassy run outside their commodious henhouse and ran to greet us, plumply feathered and clucking, one or two pausing to peck at a trough of layers' pellets. The run is protected by an electric fence to discourage foxes, and the hens showed every sign of being fortunate and well cared for.

Only if you looked closely at one individual did you notice that a wing was stunted and bare – a clue to their past. They had been among several thousand battery hens disposed of in the light of new regulations about the minimum space allowable per bird. There was a television appeal for people who might take some. An animal rescue centre at Wincanton gave temporary accommodation to a batch at a time and it was from there that these twelve had come to Mudford; skinny, almost bare of feathers, frightened and thirsty.

That was back in July. For two days they cowered inside the henhouse, afraid of the light. After a fortnight they were getting used to a free-range existence, and after eight weeks they were fully feathered. In summer they produced about a dozen eggs every day. The one I poached demonstrated how the corn in their diet produces a rich, red-gold yolk.

Under the Flightpath

Public meetings have recently been held in south-east Somerset in response to long-standing concerns about heavy road traffic in the villages. But a few days ago we visited one nearby village whose main street carried little traffic and which seemed to retain much of the gentle, secluded character attributed to it by a traveller in 1633, who commented that "by reason that it stands in a flat country it yields a goodly prospect to such as pass that way".

The River Cam or Camel flows in a deep and twisting channel between banks and stone walls and under little bridges through the heart of the village. Beside the old rectory stands a magnificent tithe barn and a little, circular dovecote. Across the road, another ancient barn, long and low, but humbler, with a dilapidated thatched roof, stands beside the lane to the church. We were at the church porch when the calm was suddenly and violently undone by the sight and fearsome sound of a Hawker Harrier directly overhead, and, to a newcomer's eye, frighteningly low in the sky, as it came in to land at the Royal Navy air station. West Camel, quaint, idyllic and relatively free of road traffic, lies directly under the flightpath.

If lorries through Templecombe merit protest, how was it that the people of West Camel accepted roaring jet aircraft with apparent equanimity? A resident smiled knowingly and explained; under planning law, being in a defined area beneath the flightpath protects the village from new building and thus from developers. She claimed that, after a short while, one became sufficiently accustomed to the noise to regard it as a price worth paying for that privilege.

Wartime Evacuees

I was sitting in a handsome house with the two brothers who had built it themselves by converting two barns on a dairy farm. On 12 November 1940, their mother had brought them and her six other children, one a baby, to this quiet corner of Somerset from bomb-stricken Coventry where they had been used to mains water, gas and electricity and living close to shops. Here, they found themselves in an isolated candle-lit cottage. There was water in a pail which had to be filled from the pump some way down the lane, and another pail, in the garden, was the only toilet facility. They had to gather wood to burn in the range for cooking and warmth, and in the copper for washing or filling the bath. It was two and a half miles on foot to the shops in Templecombe or four and a half to Wincanton. A local lad took them home from the village school, which they loved, to see his father's farm. Soon they were doing odd jobs for pocket money of half a crown a week. One of them went on to work on that same farm for over 20 years. There were two Shire horses for mowing and haulage. In summer mowing started at 5.00am so that by 11.00 the cut grass was dry for turning. Milking of fifty cows by hand took four people from 6.30 to 8.30 in the morning and from 4.00 to 6.00 in the evening. There was hedging to be done, and ditching, dung-laying and hay-making. I saw a reference hand-written for the elder brother in 1963; 'There is no job on a farm he cannot turn his hand to ... He is not afraid of hard work'. After an interview at Wells, he was granted the tenancy of a County Farm.

Fonthill

Eastwards into Wiltshire and up towards Salisbury Plain, the broad expanse of chalky downland is interrupted by the humps of tumuli and occasional wooded heights and hollows. Near Hindon, in one of the hollows, we skirted the perimeter of the elevated woods of Fonthill and found a broad, grassy ride and a roadway that penetrated the wood beside a derelict lodge. The place was deserted and the atmosphere mysterious. The only moving thing, a solitary fox that ambled across our path, seemed mildly surprised but not at all alarmed by our approach. The way leads on for almost a mile, with occasional trees, until the sense of unreality is increased as it opens into a broad, mown space which surrounds a square, Gothic tower and oratory with three lancet windows. Even today, when natural growth has had time to reassert itself and obscure the design, this landscape is evidently the result of artifice; ways had been cleared to create vistas, exotic plantings introduced and natural features enhanced to make a fairytale approach to what was once Fonthill Abbey. Nelson and Emma were here in December 1800. They had been shown the alpine garden, the American plantation, the Norwegian lawn and the encircling 12-foot wall to exclude neighbouring gentry keen on hunting. "I consider we have no right to murder animals for sport", said William Beckford, whose driven and eccentric genius made this landscape to imitate those of Poussin, and finished the west front of his stupendous folly, built in haste on a scale to rival that of Salisbury Cathedral, in the nick of time to astound the admiral and his lady.

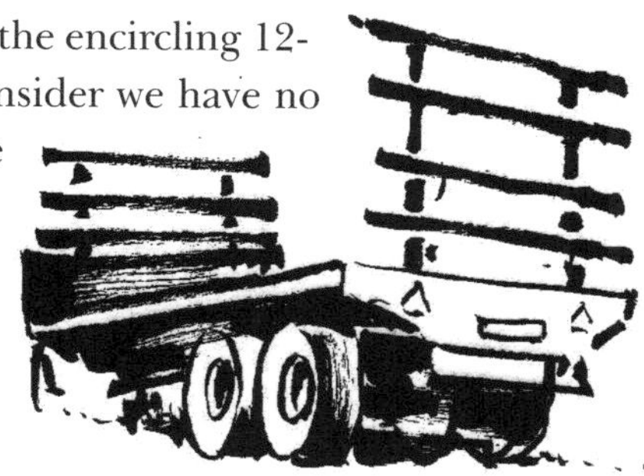

West Penwith in Winter

I first noticed the stately tower of St. Buryan's church when I looked up from the ploughing match at a nearby farm. It stood up starkly from a flat landscape in West Penwith. Friends at home in gentle, rolling South Somerset had said, even before the snows fell across Bodmin Moor, that we were mad to holiday in that far end of Cornwall in November, but we were lucky with the weather. Tonkin's Natural History of Cornwall, written in 1739, described the parish of St. Buryan in 1739 as "lying very warm on the South Sea, which, with the desire of living quiet, has induced several gentlemen to settle themselves in this remote corner of the kingdom".

We went over to the "Ancient Church of St. Buriana, Royal Peculiar and Cathedral of the West", as proclaimed in its short history and guidebook entitled The Wickedest Parish in Cornwall; we were told by a woman there that the saint, whose name is associated with strange and miraculous events, had sailed across, as legend claims for so many others, from Ireland in a coracle. The origin of the great collegiate church was a vow by Athelstan to raise a church on the site of the saint's oratory, as a thank-offering for his victory, just across the water in the Scillies, over the Danes.

At Mousehole, heavy timbers were already set across the harbour entrance as defence against the winter seas, although wet-suited surfers were still out in Whitesands Bay. The busy harbour at Newlyn was full of working vessels; it was good to watch a cheerful crew from Padstow coming in to unload their catch. A harbour-side plaque commemorates the seven-man crew of the little Newlyn lugger Mystery. In 1854, when times were hard for both fishermen and miners, rather than sell the Mystery, they sailed in her from Newlyn to Melbourne to try their luck in Australia.

A Hard Day's Work on a Dairy Farm

I went down towards Bulbarrow to a dairy farm worked by Nick Tuke, a young county tenant farmer, and his wife, Marilyn, with one helper on one day a week. Nick gets up at 4.30am, eats breakfast, and goes out with the dog to round up his Holstein cows. He is dedicated to improving his stock. His wife looks after the calves, and he maintains that her patience, attentive to each individual's condition and needs, is crucial. When the couple started farming 11 years ago, they had 50 acres and 40 cows and got 26p per litre. The average yield per cow per year was then 7,000 litres, and these figures provided a decent living.

Now they have 95 acres and 90 cows. Their work over the years has increased the yield from 7,000 litres to 10,200, but at 18.5p per litre the milk provides a less good living today than it did then. Milking takes two hours. He knows each cow and taps her number into the computer which regulates the feed ration. By 7.30am he has washed down and sterilised the milking parlour. Then, in summer, the cows go back to pasture. In winter they go into a "loose yard", a big, covered space rebedded with clean straw. Routine jobs must be done – hedging, ditching, putting slurry on the fields, attending to cows' feet. A bite of lunch is welcome. By 3.30pm it's back to the milking parlour. Paperwork takes the equivalent of a day's work each week.

Looking at the pens of carefully tended new-born calves you can see that his wife's work requires no less commitment. I asked him why they do it. He said they love a job where home and workplace are one and the same, that he likes the open air, and is passionate about raising good cows. He finishes at 8pm, eats and sleeps.

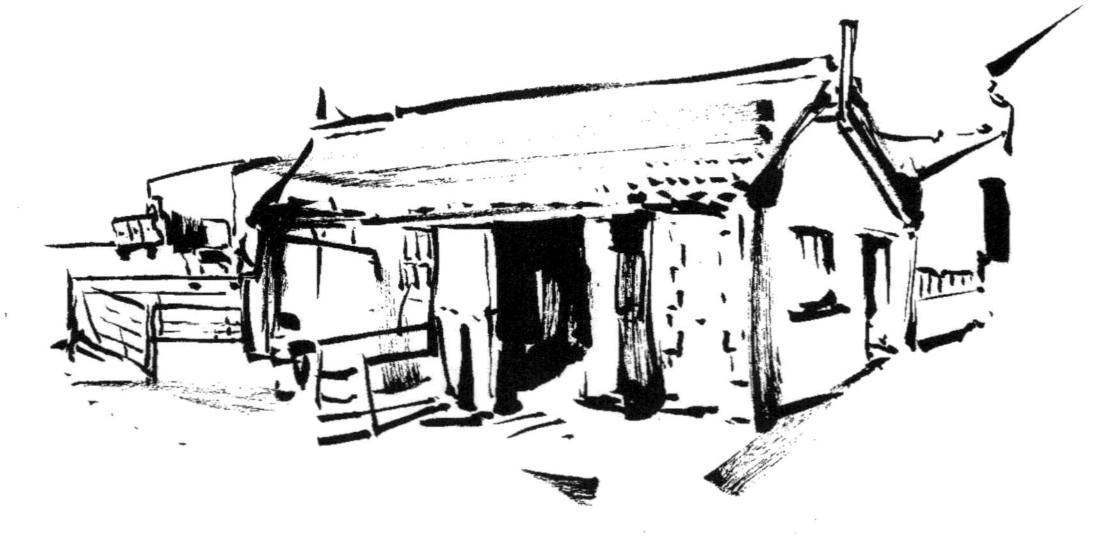

Wind-power

Gusts of wind woke us by rattling our roof tiles and snapping branches off trees, but the storms did not strike this locality, least of all our immediate and sheltered southward slopes, with anything like the force that did such destruction elsewhere.

Next day there were pictures of a recently parched Kent reservoir now brimming over and tossed like a rough sea, and forecasts that we should look for more violent extremes of weather if climate change continued unchecked. It was only a day or two later that I stood on high ground outside Castle Cary, and looked north-westwards to a steep drop down to the lowlands that stretch away for 30 miles to the sea.

The prevailing wind blows in uninterrupted (with heights like Glastonbury Tor and Brent Knoll just pimples in the flat landscape) towards the place where I stood. Wind here may be strong enough to knock over your wheelie bin, but is unlikely to rip off your roof. So local conditions enable people to regard wind as a useful and infinitely renewable resource.

They have already begun to exploit it to generate clean power. There will be a village meeting at Hadspen tomorrow to consider a proposal to set up a wind turbine as a community project with all residents as shareholders. The owner of the proposed site employs solar power and a heat-exchange system in his house, and plans to use another local resource, the pomace from his 10,000 cider-apple trees, to make methane fuel for his vehicles.

Ansford school plans to generate its own power from a wind turbine, and at the Carymoor environmental centre I saw two turbines, the larger one a 15kW version, and to my eye a fine sight with its silver mast standing up against the sky. One local resident with his own turbine, batteries and solar panels is already independent of the grid.

Wiltshire Bison

My eastward route out of Somerset climbed away from the small fields of dairy farms stocked with black and white cows, and up into a layer of thickening fog that obscured the views across wide, open Wiltshire downs, where you usually see pigs rooting about among rows of pig shelters like miniature Nissen huts. But then my turning led into a lane that took me down again, below the fog line, and a sharply etched scene materialised – bare, black winter woods flanking a green valley with a square-towered church to the right – all familiarly English. However, few of the animals at Bush farm, at the end of the valley, were English or familiar. Several bison were lounging massively in the yard. In a nearby paddock some elegant long-necked camelids stared at us. I was told that they were guanacos, from South America, relatives of the llama and the alpaca. The elk and red deer were out of sight, roaming the sloping sides of the valley or maybe hidden by the woods beyond the lake. The horned sheep in a sheltered pen were light brown Castlemilk Moorits, developed on the Castlemilk estate in Dumfriesshire from primitive breeds – some say to please the laird's eye, as they complement the colours in his landscape. But it was the bison I had come to see. This is the animal that used to roam the American plains in vast numbers. It fed, clothed and sheltered the native Americans until hunted almost to extinction by Europeans. At our farmers market, I had learned the merits of bison meat (low in calories, fat and cholesterol) and had visited this farm before, but it was still extraordinary to see that legendary shape, remembered from the cinema screen, on home ground – the great, hanging head and the humped shoulder clad in shaggy fur – and to marvel at the sheer size of the adult male. He can grow to a length of 3.5 metres and stand 2 metres tall at the shoulder, weighing nearly 1,000 kg.

Steep Holm, The Bristol Channel

A rough and windy day at the turn of the year makes me think of Steep Holm, the rocky outcrop that stands up from the swirling tidal currents of the Bristol Channel. Even in summer, the scheduled trips of the Bristol Queen from Weston to Steep Holm are vulnerable to last-minute cancellation because of unsafe conditions, and in winter only a few hardy and experienced enthusiasts, members of the Kenneth Allsop Trust which owns the island, make occasional forays in a little boat called Skylark. So the flora and fauna have the place largely to themselves. A meticulous natural history survey records their status annually. There are species of flora that would not normally be expected to occur on a rocky island in this part of the world, among them the wild peony, wild leek, alexander, henbane and hemlock, whose presence is thought to be connected with that of the priory.

In September, after a calm crossing, we watched archaeologists dig at the priory site, and heard that Augustinian "black canons" lived, prayed, built, died and were buried here in the 12th century. The plants are probably evidence that they practised the medieval herbalist's art. In the 14th century, when the island was a "coney island", supplying rabbit skins and meat to the mainland, the resident warreners made their homes in the ruins of the priory.

There had been earlier inhabitants: Romans, who built a semaphore signal station, and Vikings making a base for sorties across the water. The farmhouse and cottage are evidence of agriculture and fishing in the 18th and 19th centuries.

The cottage was later used by workmen employed in building the inn, now a ruin down by the shingle beach, where there was hope of rich profits due to immunity from mainland licensing laws and the chance to purchase liquor from passing merchant ships without paying excise duty.

But it is probably the birdlife that chiefly concerns many of those who know the island best and care about it most. The RSPB has asked for a full survey of the seabird population, and the island's report for Spring 2008 recorded 91 cormorant nests, a slight drop from the previous year, a relatively stable gull population (with a count of 1,353 herring gulls), but an "abysmal" record of migrants. We look forward to the new spring life-cycle, with mild weather and a flat sea, when the boat sets out again.

Sedgemoor and Quantocks

Across the Sedgemoor flats the scene was all in shades of grey; dark grey willows lining the streams and causeways against a pale grey sky, and the tower of Westonzoyland church, a blue-grey column in the mist across the blank space of the site of the battlefield. We were heading for Holford, a village that lies just below the wooded fringes of the Quantock Hills. A triangle of rough grass in a clearing there is called the bowling green, because, they say, Huguenot settlers used to play boules there. From close to the bowling green we took a wide track, which the map called "the great road", leading up through thick growth of oak and holly. The footing was uneven: rubble and stone slabs, relics of the ancient carriageway mostly covered with wet oak leaves. Steep-sided gullies, combes and clefts – Holford Combe, Hodder's Combe and Willoughby Cleeve – are carved out of the hillside and there are fast-running streams crossed by stepping-stones. Beside the track, shattered limbs of oak trees were decaying in the undergrowth. We heard few sounds except the hollow echo of a woodpecker drilling. Further up the hillside, the vegetation changes; oak begins to give way to birch, there is bracken and gorse, and you start to be aware of open space not far ahead on the Quantock heights.

We emerged from the cover of the woods on to the slopes of Longstone Hill, and reached a group of pines planted as a memorial to Holford's war dead. We had looked forward to the view from here, where you can see around the full 360 degrees. In her Alfoxden Journal, Dorothy Wordsworth records her impressions as she emerges from the woods and sees: "The Welsh hills capped by a huge range of tumultuous white clouds ... the distant prospect on the land-side, islanded with sunshine." But as we looked round we could still see only shades of grey – just the darkest marking the rectangular shape of Hinkley Point nuclear power station.

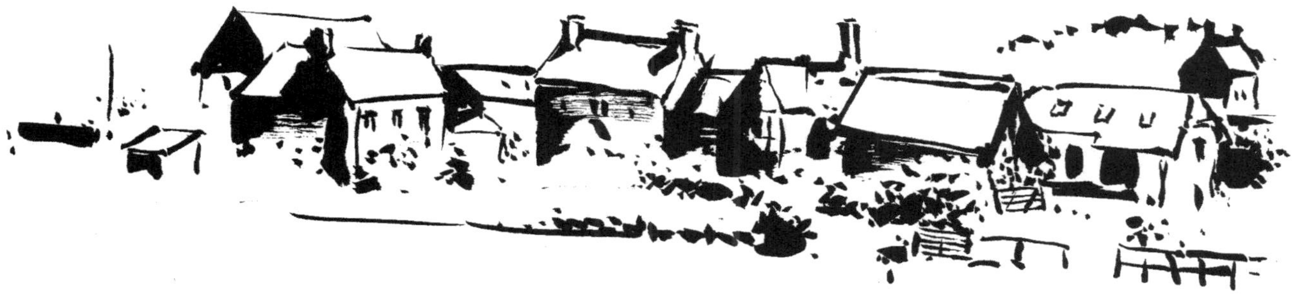

Briantspuddle

We were at a folk concert in one of Dorset's most singular village halls – long, low and thatched – that took us by a winding lane and an ancient bridge over the river Piddle to Briantspuddle. And it was the sight of a striking set of portraits in the hall, painted, it transpired, by a daughter of Sir Ernest Debenham (of Debenham and Freebody), that led to conversations which indicated what a remarkable place this is.

Until the first world war, it was a village of 12 cottages, mostly ancient and thatched, several of which survive. Then Sir Ernest – an idealistic reformer with a vision of increasing agricultural production, attracting people back to work the land, developing scientific methods and making rural Dorset self-sufficient in food production – bought land in the valley and set out to create an ideal agricultural community. The portraits are of members of his family and workers on the estate. By 1919 the estate covered 10,000 acres and was ahead of its time, self-sufficient in electric power, with its own transport depot, a dairy with a sophisticated bacterial laboratory, steam wagons and a pumping station. For his workers, he built spacious, well-appointed arts and crafts dwellings, employing local crafts and design sympathetic to the local tradition. Each house is substantial and pleasing to the eye, and no two are the same. The overall effect is harmonious. There are wide grass verges and the houses are generously spaced, with 30 metres or so between dwellings and plenty of trees to vary the scene.

Today Briantspuddle is a testament to a grand ideal only partly realised. In the event, agricultural development led not to Debenham's hoped-for increase in the number of folk working the land but to a steep and continuing decrease. The people who live in his cottages now are not farm workers.

An Isolated Village

The Mendip foothills north of Bruton can be steep and sudden. When I first went that way, I had to engage first gear in an elderly Austin to grind painfully up the last gradient to Batcombe. But down below lies Batcombe Vale and at its heart, largely unnoticed, the isolated hamlet of Spargrove – mill, farm, ancient tithe-barn and manor – beside the river Alham. I went back there after many years, and, as before, there was no sound until I got close enough to hear the roar of the water through the empty mill chamber, and no other creature, man or beast, to be seen. It felt like a place apart.

The following day, I was to meet someone who, as a child in the 1950s, had been part of the tiny community that lived at Spargrove. Her grandparents had at first lived in the manor, on a site retaining traces of early bank and moat defences. She, her brother and their parents lived in the mill house, while a few yards up the slope, in Lower Spargrove Farm, lived seven brothers and sisters of a family that had owned Spargrove land since 1800. They lived a secluded life, never engaging much with outside folk, but welcoming my friend and her brother into their home after school if their mother was still out milking the cows.

There were few visitors in those days, except the milk lorry and the postman, and a man in a black car with running boards who fetched the two children to and from school (two teachers, one for the big ones and one for the little ones, and regular visits by the nit nurse). The fishmonger came on Friday and left bits for the tribe of cats at the farm. The seven siblings went on in their own way, withdrawn from the march of progress, until 1988, when a fire raked the house (still candlelit) and killed 80-year-old Mary and 77-year-old Chris. None of the family survives today.

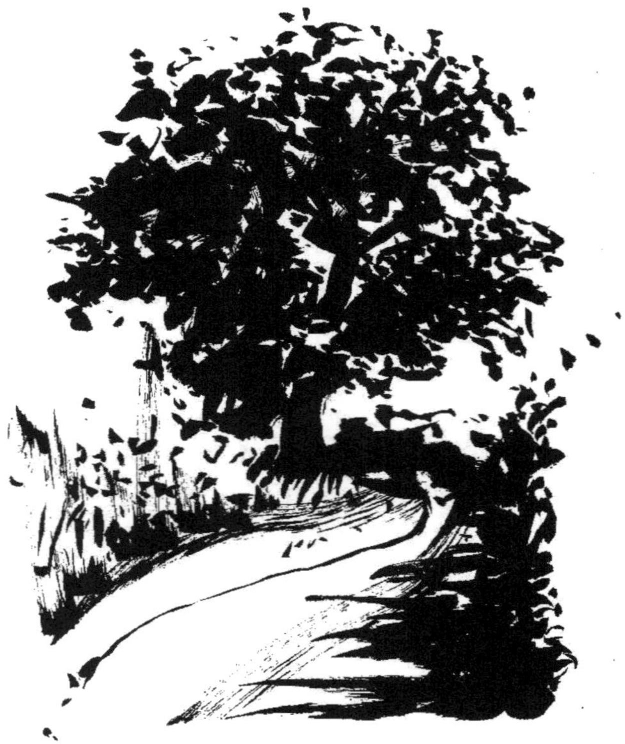

Hamdon Hill

Getting down towards the foot of Hamdon Hill, we saw a man at work on a thatched roof in the village below. He moved to and fro across the slanting surface, raking, tamping, placing new bundles of straw, and deftly shifting his ladder to apparently precarious angles with the sure-footed poise of a skilled athlete. And there was already enough of his new, pale-coloured thatch to show how right the completed roof would be to top the house, bearing the date of 1605. Long and low with mullioned windows, it was built all of hamstone (variously described as golden or biscuit-coloured) quarried from the hill where we had been walking.

The surface of Hamdon Hill, ringed by three miles of defensive ramparts, is everywhere shaped and scarred by its history as a fortified settlement from Neolithic to Roman times, and as a source of building stone since quarrying began there, it is reckoned, 2,000 years ago. Commercial quarrying still goes on, though much less than in the Victorian era when more than 200 small quarries were operating. A vertical cliff face, remnant of earlier workings, shows the layers of red-gold stone, varied here and there with darker streaks, and split or gouged by hand tools – pick, wedge, hammer and adze. The great house of Montacute, and the village beside it, as well as other whole villages close to the quarries, were built of hamstone, whose makeup of shells and crystals gives it its characteristic golden glow when sunlit.

Mills and farmhouses right across the region and even humbler dwellings, made of whichever stone was available nearby, are often given hamstone detail around doors and windows which makes a contrast with the local quarry's prevailing grey and gives a touch of richer quality.

Mells River

The roads west of Frome negotiate steep and sudden Mendip country, bare heights, streams, and lushly wooded hollows. Round one bend, the eye was led to a graceful hilltop group of stone buildings topped by a slender church spire. This was the village of Whatley. Then, dropping down through the woods, we came at once upon a stark contrast: the giant, modern industrial plant of a quarry which extracts limestone rock to make roads. We were heading for the Mells river in the cleft of its deep valley, and on our way caught sight of Mells village down below us, a famously picturesque scene, with the Elizabethan manor next door to the perpendicular church, and a medieval street of honey-coloured cottages. Mells on an autumn Sunday morning had an air of untroubled rural calm and gentle relaxation. But a short distance along the bridle-way beside the river we came upon relics of the place's earlier industrial character. At first, as we left the road, we noticed only the wooded slope on our left, the slow, green river curving beside the track on our right, and the occasional couple walking their dogs. The way soon enters a chasm, a miniature Cheddar gorge, enclosed by sheer walls of rock. There are mossy trees leaning out over the water, and overgrown fragments of ruined buildings, now almost absorbed into the natural scenery, relics of the days of sweat and toil, one with a chimney like those of the derelict Cornish tin-mines, all tangled with branches and creeper. There used to be iron foundries in this valley, as well as the factories of the best edge-tool makers in England, breweries, and fulling mills for the cloth business when Frome was called the Manchester of the south. We passed the spot where the flow of the river quickens over the remains of a weir, and a small, vigorous waterfall splashes out of the rock on the far bank, evidence of the force of underground streams that thread through the hard limestone.

Quaker Settlement

It was a fortnight since we had stood in the fields outside Ilchester and looked at the track that leads in a straight line from the packhorse bridge there towards the village of Long Load. And now I was looking back from the other end of that track, and standing beside the much more ancient and substantial bridge that carries the road from Ilchester to Langport across the River Yeo. This one is said to date from the 15th century. Its construction is massively solid and there are five arches. It took me 32 paces to get from one end to the other and five to cross its carriageway. The winding river is in a deep gully here with embankments on each side which are high, but not high enough always to contain the river. A man standing outside his roadside house pointed across Kingsmoor, a desolate looking tract on this grey day, towards a wide sheet of water alongside the river and a pumping station – relatively recent features of the continuing struggle to manage the interaction between land and water. He said that Kingsmoor was sometimes like a sea behind his house, but that in his time the water had never quite got in. He directed me to Long Sutton, a mile or so north, on slightly higher ground, where fine buildings – tall, perpendicular church, schoolhouse and handsome dwellings – are grouped around a village green, but I went on to look for the Quaker Meeting House. In 1655 'The Lord sent severall of his faithfull ... into the County of Somerset'. Some settled here. The lovely symmetrical Meeting House bears the inscription 'Ex dono Willm Steell. Anno Domini 1717.' There are seven straight rows of small, identical gravestones in a grassy burial ground. Over the hedge, a Charolais bull was quietly steaming.

Dartmoor Sheep in the Cold

When the worst of the snowfall was over, I went out across the marsh to hear how the Greyface Dartmoor sheep were faring in the winter weather. The road was slushy and the ice on the horse pond had begun to crack, but the tops of the trees and hedges were still frosted white. As natives of Dartmoor, these sheep are well-equipped to cope with the cold. They can dig down into the snow, though the amount of grass they can get needs to be supplemented by increased rations of dry feed. After shearing in spring, their fleeces are three-quarters of the way back to their full, shaggy, outer thickness, impervious to cold and wet. If you press down into their broad backs, the silky inner layers, close to the skin, are warm and dry to the touch.

During his coffee break, indoors and warm, the man tending the flock these past weeks told me more about sheep in winter. While most cattle go in from the fields from late October, sheep, except ewes at lambing time, generally stay outside whatever the weather. He reminisced about really hard winters in 1963, 1978 and 1979, when there were helicopter drops to some of the more inaccessible villages near here, and told me his father, who had looked after sheep up in the Cotswolds, reckoned it was not until the snow reached the tops of the dry-stone walls that he needed to go and see if any sheep needed to be dug out. In extreme conditions, an animal might be located by the sight of its steamy breath rising from a blow-hole. And a useful skill in winter was the construction of makeshift shelters from hurdles.

By comparison with the world he described, conditions this year in South Somerset had, when we spoke, been relatively mild. But even so there had been difficulties. The long drought in summer limiting the growth of grass has meant that hay is in short supply and expensive. The small local mills that supplied feed to farms and farmers they knew well, have mostly gone, so now supplies have to come from further afield, when maybe roads and lanes are icy. But for these Dartmoor sheep domiciled in Somerset, drinking water had been the real problem. Their increased dry feed, including oats, barley, sugar-beet and molasses, requires them to drink sufficient water morning and evening to avoid harm to their kidneys. But it has been hard to get the water to the fields and into their buckets before it has frozen solid in its five-gallon plastic drums. As I write, there has been more and heavier snow.

Christmas Spirit at Cary Marsh

Years ago I went to Maiden Bradley, in Wiltshire, to see how people were encouraging tree sparrows to return to an area where they had hardly been seen for years. Wide headlands were being left around the ploughed fields and the right feed spread. And now I was walking along the old drove road west of Castle Cary into the wide, watery space of Cary Moor with two folk equipped with binoculars and a telescope. They too hoped to see tree sparrows. Small flocks of birds darted across between the trees ahead of us. They were at once confidently identified by my companions: chaffinches, reed buntings and yellowhammers but no tree sparrows, although between 15 and 25 are now resident in this wetland, brought back by the establishment of the Cary Marsh nature reserve.

Streams have been diverted, ponds dug, and 60,000 reeds planted to make a reed bed. Shrubs and trees native to the area have been planted to create woodland, and a big field has been sown with crops that provide the winter forage that attracts the seed eaters: tree sparrows, yellowhammers and reed buntings among them. The reed bed, I was told, has successfully brought reed warblers to breed here, with 12 pairs in 2010, and a sighting of a juvenile water rail is proof that these secretive birds, too, have bred.

On Christmas morning, the roads were icy and impassable to traffic, and snow covered the frozen fields. Anxious about the birds' food source, my companions had trudged three miles to the reserve, their breath freezing in the temperature of -12C. It struck me that they were in the spirit of King Wenceslas and the page, though they were carrying not bread, wine or pine logs, but sacks of grain for the birds' breakfast. And grateful flocks swarmed in.

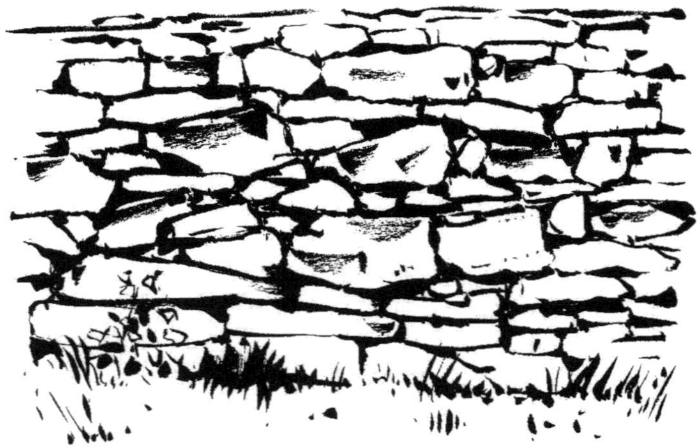

Flagon Press

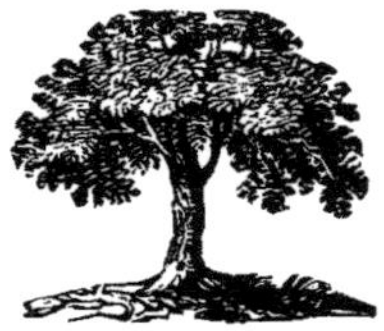

Flagon Press is the imprint belonging to James Crowden Publishing and its aim is to publish local books with the same ethos as local food. In other words, local subjects for local books, local writers, local designers, local printers, alternative low key marketing, low carbon footprint distribution to local bookshops and other alternative outlets. The main graphic designer is the artist Andrew Crane of Whitelackington near Ilminster who now lives near Hadrian's Wall. Two of the covers already used by Flagon Press are from mixed media textile works by Alice Crane of Wambrook.

James Crowden's first book *Blood, Earth & Medicine* was a hot lead monotype/letter press book printed on a 5½ ton Heidelberg by the Parrett Press in 1991. The same Heidelberg printing press has now moved a few miles to Ilminster and is now being used by Rose Mills Print. Other books for Flagon Press have been printed and bound by Remous of Milborne Port on the Dorset/Somerset border or Butler, Tanner and Dennis of Frome.

Other Flagon Press titles include *The Last Broomsquire, The Devon Food Book, Literary Somerset, Dorset Coast, Dorset Footsteps, Coastlines, Chasing the Light, The Bad Winter, Lewesdon Hill* and *We Have Heard Ravens.*

James Crowden and his team of designers believe that each book is an individual work of art that should arise organically and be crafted, not mass produced. Books are to be savoured …and enjoyed like an artisan Calvados or Cider Brandy…

www.james-crowden.co.uk